Network Safety

EC-Council | Press

This title maps to

Network | 5™

Australia • Brazil • Japan • Korea • Mexico • Singapore • Spain • United Kingdom • United States

Network Safety
EC-Council | Press

Course Technology/Cengage Learning Staff:

Vice President, Career and Professional Editorial: Dave Garza

Director of Learning Solutions: Matthew Kane

Executive Editor: Stephen Helba

Managing Editor: Marah Bellegarde

Editorial Assistant: Meghan Orvis

Vice President, Career and Professional Marketing: Jennifer Ann Baker

Marketing Director: Deborah Yarnell

Marketing Manager: Erin Coffin

Marketing Coordinator: Shanna Gibbs

Production Director: Carolyn Miller

Production Manager: Andrew Crouth

Content Project Manager: Brooke Greenhouse

Senior Art Director: Jack Pendleton

EC-Council:

President | EC-Council: Sanjay Bavisi

Sr. Director US | EC-Council: Steven Graham

© 2011 EC-Council

ALL RIGHTS RESERVED. No part of this work covered by the copyright herein may be reproduced, transmitted, stored, or used in any form or by any means graphic, electronic, or mechanical, including but not limited to photocopying, recording, scanning, digitizing, taping, Web distribution, information networks, or information storage and retrieval systems, except as permitted under Section 107 or 108 of the 1976 United States Copyright Act, without the prior written permission of the publisher.

For product information and technology assistance, contact us at
Cengage Learning Customer & Sales Support, 1-800-354-9706

For permission to use material from this text or product,
submit all requests online at **www.cengage.com/permissions**.
Further permissions questions can be e-mailed to
permissionrequest@cengage.com

Library of Congress Control Number: 2010926145

ISBN-13: 978-1-4354-8377-4

ISBN-10: 1-4354-8377-4

Cengage Learning
5 Maxwell Drive
Clifton Park, NY 12065-2919
USA

Cengage Learning is a leading provider of customized learning solutions with office locations around the globe, including Singapore, the United Kingdom, Australia, Mexico, Brazil, and Japan. Locate your local office at: **international.cengage.com/region**

Cengage Learning products are represented in Canada by Nelson Education, Ltd.

For more learning solutions, please visit our corporate website at **www.cengage.com**

NOTICE TO THE READER

Cengage Learning and EC-Council do not warrant or guarantee any of the products described herein or perform any independent analysis in connection with any of the product information contained herein. Cengage Learning and EC-Council do not assume, and expressly disclaim, any obligation to obtain and include information other than that provided to it by the manufacturer. The reader is expressly warned to consider and adopt all safety precautions that might be indicated by the activities described herein and to avoid all potential hazards. By following the instructions contained herein, the reader willingly assumes all risks in connection with such instructions. Cengage Learning and EC-Council make no representations or warranties of any kind, including but not limited to, the warranties of fitness for particular purpose or merchantability, nor are any such representations implied with respect to the material set forth herein, and Cengage Learning and EC-Council take no responsibility with respect to such material. Cengage Learning and EC-Council shall not be liable for any special, consequential, or exemplary damages resulting, in whole or part, from the readers' use of, or reliance upon, this material.

Printed in the United States of America
1 2 3 4 5 6 7 12 11 10

Brief Table of Contents

TABLE OF CONTENTS v

PREFACE ix

CHAPTER 1
Foundations of Networks 1-1

CHAPTER 2
Network Components 2-1

CHAPTER 3
LAN Technologies 3-1

CHAPTER 4
Installation of Basic Hardware Components 4-1

CHAPTER 5
Network Connectivity 5-1

CHAPTER 6
Wireless Networking 6-1

CHAPTER 7
Networking Environment 7-1

CHAPTER 8
Troubleshooting 8-1

INDEX I-1

Table of Contents

PREFACE ix

CHAPTER 1
Foundations of Networks 1-1
    Objectives 1-1
    Key Terms 1-1
    Case Study 1-2
    Introduction to Foundations of Networks 1-2
    What Is a Network? 1-2
    Need for a Network 1-2
    Client, Workstation, and Server 1-3
        Client 1-3
        Workstation 1-3
        Server 1-3
    Different Network Models 1-3
        Peer-To-Peer 1-3
        Client-Server 1-4
        Mainframe 1-4
    Types of Networks 1-4
        Local Area Network (LAN) 1-4
        Wide Area Network (WAN) 1-6
        Metropolitan Area Network (MAN) 1-6
    Various Network Topologies 1-6
        Ring Topology 1-6
        Mesh Topology 1-6
        Star Topology 1-7
        Tree Bus Topology 1-7
        Linear Bus Topology 1-7
    Chapter Summary 1-9
    Review Questions 1-9
    Hands-On Projects 1-10

CHAPTER 2
Network Components 2-1
    Objectives 2-1
    Key Terms 2-1
    Introduction to Network Components 2-2
    Network Components 2-2
        Repeaters 2-2
        Hubs 2-2
        Bridges 2-3
        Routers 2-3
        Switches 2-4
        Gateways 2-5
        Brouters 2-5
    Types of Networking Cables 2-5
    Media Connectors 2-6
        RJ-11 (Registered Jack) 2-6
        RJ-45 (Registered Jack) 2-6
        IEEE 1394 2-6
        USB 2-6
    How to Choose a Cable 2-6
    Chapter Summary 2-7
    Review Questions 2-8
    Hands-On Projects 2-9

CHAPTER 3
LAN Technologies 3-1

- Objectives 3-1
- Key Terms 3-1
- Case Study 3-2
- Introduction to LAN Technologies 3-2
- Ethernet and Its Characteristics 3-2
- Physical Characteristics 3-3
- Different Categories in Ethernet 3-3
- Baseband Ethernet 3-4
  - 10Base5 3-4
  - 10Base2 3-4
  - 10BaseT 3-4
- Broadband Ethernet 3-5
  - 10Broad36 3-5
- Ethernet Cable Types 3-5
  - Twisted-Pair Cable 3-6
  - Coaxial Cable 3-6
  - Fiber-Optic Cable 3-6
- Other Types of Ethernet LAN 3-7
- Virtual Private Network 3-7
- Connecting to a VPN Using Windows 2000 3-8
- Chapter Summary 3-9
- Review Questions 3-9
- Hands-On Projects 3-10

CHAPTER 4
Installation of Basic Hardware Components 4-1

- Objectives 4-1
- Key Terms 4-1
- Case Study 4-2
- Introduction to Installation of Basic Hardware Components 4-2
- Basic Hardware Components 4-2
- Installing a CPU 4-3
- Installing a Motherboard 4-3
  - Configuring a Motherboard 4-3
- Installing Power Supply 4-4
- Installing a Hard Drive 4-4
- Installing Floppy and CD/DVD Drives 4-5
- Legacy Devices 4-5
  - Interrupt Request Line Assignments 4-6
  - Direct Memory Access 4-6
  - Input/Output Addresses 4-7
  - Configuring IDE/ATA Devices 4-7
  - SCSI Devices 4-8
  - Safe BIOS Settings 4-8
  - CMOS 4-9
- Understanding Ports 4-9
  - Data Cables 4-9
  - Connectors 4-10
- Detecting Hardware Devices 4-10
  - Using Device Manager 4-10
- Chapter Summary 4-12
- Review Questions 4-12
- Hands-On Projects 4-14

CHAPTER 5
Network Connectivity 5-1

    Objectives 5-1

    Key Terms 5-1

    Case Study 5-2

    Setting Up a Small Network 5-2

    Connecting Computers 5-2
        Hardware Installation 5-2
        Software Installation 5-3

    IP Addressing 5-3
        Verifying the Connection 5-4
        Assigning an IP Address 5-4
        Adding Computers to a Workgroup 5-4

    Network Services 5-5
        DHCP 5-5
        WINS 5-6
        DNS 5-6

    Deciding on a Network Architecture 5-7

    Internet Access Technology 5-7
        xDSL 5-8
        Broadband Cable 5-9
        Wireless 5-9
        Dial-Up Connection 5-9

    File Sharing 5-9
        Types of File Sharing 5-9
        How to Share a Folder 5-10
        Configuring Shared Folder Permissions 5-10

    Chapter Summary 5-10

    Review Questions 5-11

    Hands-On Projects 5-12

CHAPTER 6
Wireless Networking 6-1

    Objectives 6-1

    Key Terms 6-1

    Case Study 6-2

    Introduction to Wireless Networking 6-2

    Wireless Networks 6-2
        Expanding the IEEE Standard 6-3

    Types of Wireless Networks 6-4
        WLAN 6-4
        WPAN 6-4
        WMAN 6-5
        WWAN 6-5

    Wireless Network Requirements 6-5
        Antennas 6-6
        SSIDs 6-6
        Access Point Positioning 6-6
        WEP 6-6

    Setting Up a Wireless Network 6-7
        Connecting an Adapter 6-7
        Installing a Driver 6-7
        Accessing a WLAN 6-8

    Advantages and Disadvantages of Wireless Networks 6-8

    Chapter Summary 6-8

    Review Questions 6-9

    Hands-On Projects 6-10

CHAPTER 7
Networking Environment 7-1
- Objective 7-1
- Key Terms 7-1
- Case Study 7-2
- Introduction to Networking Environment 7-2
- Introduction to Intranet 7-2
  - Managing an Intranet 7-2
- Internet and Intranet Differences 7-2
  - Intranet Advantages 7-2
- How an Intranet Operates 7-3
  - Inside an Intranet 7-4
  - Checklist for Building an Intranet 7-4
- Introduction to Extranet 7-5
- Internet and Extranet Differences 7-5
  - Extranet Advantages 7-5
- How an Extranet Operates 7-6
- Intranet and Extranet Differences 7-7
- Chapter Summary 7-8
- Review Questions 7-8
- Hands-On Projects 7-9

CHAPTER 8
Troubleshooting 8-1
- Objectives 8-1
- Introduction to Troubleshooting 8-1
- Hardware Errors and Their Codes 8-1
- Troubleshooting Guidelines 8-2
- Network Connectivity Issues 8-2
  - Testing Network Connectivity 8-2
  - File and Printer Connectivity 8-3
- Motherboard Failure 8-3
  - Response 8-3
- Central Processor Unit Failure 8-3
  - Checking the CPU Fan 8-4
- Power Supply Failure 8-4
- Video/Display Failure 8-4
- Memory Chip Failure 8-4
- CD-ROM Failure 8-4
- Chapter Summary 8-5
- Review Questions 8-5

INDEX I-1

Preface

Hacking and electronic crimes sophistication has grown at an exponential rate in recent years. In fact, recent reports have indicated that cyber crime already surpasses the illegal drug trade! Unethical hackers better known as *black hats* are preying on information systems of government, corporate, public, and private networks and are constantly testing the security mechanisms of these organizations to the limit with the sole aim of exploiting it and profiting from the exercise. High profile crimes have proven that the traditional approach to computer security is simply not sufficient, even with the strongest perimeter, properly configured defense mechanisms like firewalls, intrusion detection, and prevention systems, strong end-to-end encryption standards, and anti-virus software. Hackers have proven their dedication and ability to systematically penetrate networks all over the world. In some cases *black hats* may be able to execute attacks so flawlessly that they can compromise a system, steal everything of value, and completely erase their tracks in less than 20 minutes!

The EC-Council Press is dedicated to stopping hackers in their tracks.

About EC-Council

The International Council of Electronic Commerce Consultants, better known as EC-Council was founded in late 2001 to address the need for well-educated and certified information security and e-business practitioners. EC-Council is a global, member-based organization comprised of industry and subject matter experts all working together to set the standards and raise the bar in information security certification and education.

EC-Council first developed the *Certified Ethical Hacker,* C|EH program. The goal of this program is to teach the methodologies, tools, and techniques used by hackers. Leveraging the collective knowledge from hundreds of subject matter experts, the C|EH program has rapidly gained popularity around the globe and is now delivered in over 70 countries by over 450 authorized training centers. Over 80,000 information security practitioners have been trained.

C|EH is the benchmark for many government entities and major corporations around the world. Shortly after C|EH was launched, EC-Council developed the *Certified Security Analyst,* E|CSA. The goal of the E|CSA program is to teach groundbreaking analysis methods that must be applied while conducting advanced penetration testing. E|CSA leads to the *Licensed Penetration Tester,* L|PT status. The *Computer Hacking Forensic Investigator,* C|HFI was formed with the same design methodologies above and has become a global standard in certification for computer forensics. EC-Council through its impervious network of professionals, and huge industry following has developed various other programs in information security and e-business. EC-Council Certifications are viewed as the essential certifications needed where standard configuration and security policy courses fall short. Providing a true, hands-on, tactical approach to security, individuals armed with the knowledge disseminated by EC-Council programs are securing networks around the world and beating the hackers at their own game.

About the EC-Council | Press

The EC-Council | Press was formed in late 2008 as a result of a cutting edge partnership between global information security certification leader, EC-Council and leading global academic publisher, Cengage Learning. This partnership marks a revolution in academic textbooks and courses of study in Information Security, Computer Forensics, Disaster Recovery, and End-User Security. By identifying the essential topics and content of EC-Council professional certification programs, and repurposing this world class content to fit academic programs, the EC-Council | Press was formed. The academic community is now able to incorporate this powerful cutting edge content into new and existing Information Security programs. By closing the gap between academic study and professional certification, students and instructors are able to leverage the power of rigorous academic focus and high demand industry certification. The EC-Council | Press is set to revolutionize global information security programs and ultimately create a new breed of practitioners capable of combating the growing epidemic of cybercrime and the rising threat of cyber-war.

Network Safety

Network Safety from EC-Council Press, provides the basic core knowledge on how infrastructure enables a working environment. It is intended for those in an office environment and for the home user who wants to optimize resource utilization, share infrastructure and make the best of technology and the convenience it offers. Topics include foundations of networks, networking components, wireless networks, basic hardware components, the networking environment and connectivity as well as troubleshooting. The book also prepares readers to take and succeed on the Network|5 certification exam from EC-Council.

Chapter Contents

Chapter 1, *Foundations of Networks*, defines the basic terminology of networks and demonstrates how networks can be used. Chapter 2, *Network Components*, introduces common components necessary when setting up different network infrastructures and outlines how to choose the proper cable for specific networking scenarios. Chapter 3, *LAN Technologies*, defines and describes the different types of Ethernet networking technologies. Chapter 4, *Installation of Basic Hardware Components*, introduces and defines the basic hardware components of a computer and how to install them. Chapter 5, *Network Connectivity*, describes how to set up a small network, choosing the appropriate network service and provides information on various Internet access technologies. Chapter 6, *Wireless Networking*, provides an overview of wireless networking and different types of wireless networks. The hardware requirements of a wireless environment are explored, setting up and connecting a wireless network is explained, and the advantages and disadvantages of wireless networking are discussed. Chapter 7. *Networking Environment*, presents an overview and compares different networking environments. Chapter 8, *Troubleshooting*, provides a set of strategies that can be used to define and resolve problems.

Chapter Features

Many features are included in each chapter and all are designed to enhance the learner's learning experience. Features include:

- *Objectives* begin each chapter and focus the learner on the most important concepts in the chapter.
- *Key Terms* are designed to familiarize the learner with terms that will be used within the chapter.
- *Case Studies*, found throughout the chapter, present a short scenario followed by questions that challenge the learner to arrive at an answer or solution to the problem presented.
- *Chapter Summary*, at the end of each chapter, serves as a review of the key concepts covered in the chapter.
- *Review Questions* allow the learner to test their comprehension of the chapter content.
- *Hands-On Projects* encourage the learner to apply the knowledge they have gained after finishing the chapter.

Additional Instructor Resources

Free to all instructors who adopt the *Network Safety* book for their courses is a complete package of instructor resources. These resources are available from the Course Technology web site, *www.cengage.com/coursetechnology*, by going to the product page for this book in the online catalog, click on the Companion Site on the Faculty side; click on any of the Instructor Resources in the left navigation and login to access the files. Once you accept the license agreement, the selected files will be displayed.

Resources include:

- *Instructor Manual*: This manual includes course objectives and additional information to help your instruction.
- *ExamView Testbank*: This Windows-based testing software helps instructors design and administer tests and pre-tests. In addition to generating tests that can be printed and administered, this full-featured program has an online testing component that allows students to take tests at the computer and have their exams automatically graded.

- *PowerPoint Presentations*: This book comes with a set of Microsoft PowerPoint slides for each chapter. These slides are meant to be used as a teaching aid for classroom presentations, to be made available to students for chapter review, or to be printed for classroom distribution. Instructors are also at liberty to add their own slides.
- *Labs*: Additional Hands-on Activities to provide additional practice for your students.
- *Assessment Activities*: Additional assessment opportunities including discussion questions, writing assignments, internet research activities, and homework assignments along with a final cumulative project.
- *Final Exam*: Provides a comprehensive assessment of *Network Safety* content.

Cengage Learning Information Security Community Site

This site was created for learners and instructors to find out about the latest in information security news and technology.

Visit *community.cengage.com/infosec* to:

- Learn what's new in information security through live news feeds, videos and podcasts.
- Connect with your peers and security experts through blogs and forums.
- Browse our online catalog.

How to Become Network|5 Certified

Network|5 certification is appropriate for the office worker or the home user. Today's office workers are increasingly called upon to become self reliant and competent to deal with routine operational tasks. Contemporary job profiles seek greater knowledge and productivity factors from the average office user. What these knowledge workers of today need to herald in an integrated environment is the basic core knowledge of to know how infrastructure enables a work environment. As a home user, who banks online, accesses work online, subscribes to a broadband connection, Network|5 certification is needed to stay abreast in this networked world.

Network | 5 Certification exams are available through Prometric Prime . To finalize your certification after your training, you must:

1. Purchase an exam voucher from the EC-Council Community Site at Cengage: *www.cengage.com/community/eccouncil*.
2. Speak with your Instructor or Professor about scheduling an exam session, or visit the EC-Council Community Site referenced above for more information.
3. Take and pass the Network | 5 certification examination with a score of 70% or better.

About Our Other EC-Council | Press Products

Network Defense Series

The EC-Council | Press *Network Defense* series is intended for those studying to become system administrators, network administrators and anyone who is interested in network security technologies. This series is designed to educate learners, from a vendor neutral standpoint, how to defend the networks they manage. This series covers the fundamental skills in evaluating internal and external threats to network security, design, and how to enforce network level security policies, and ultimately protect an organization's information. Covering a broad range of topics from secure network fundamentals, protocols & analysis, standards and policy, hardening infrastructure, to configuring IPS, IDS and firewalls, bastion host and honeypots, among many other topics, learners completing this series will have a full understanding of defensive measures taken to secure their organizations information.

Books in Series:
- *Network Defense: Fundamentals and Protocols*/1435483553
- *Network Defense: Security Policy and Threats*/1435483561
- *Network Defense: Perimeter Defense Mechanisms*/143548357X
- *Network Defense: Securing and Troubleshooting Network Operating Systems*/1435483588
- *Network Defense: Security and Vulnerability Assessment*/1435483596

Ethical Hacking and Countermeasures Series

The EC-Council | Press *Ethical Hacking and Countermeasures* series is intended for those studying to become security officers, auditors, security professionals, site administrators, and anyone who is concerned about, or responsible for the integrity of the network infrastructure The series includes a broad base of topics in offensive network security, ethical hacking, as well as network defense and countermeasures. The content of this program is designed to immerse the learner into an interactive environment where they will be shown how to scan, test, hack and secure information systems. A wide variety of tools, virus', and malware is presented in this course providing a complete understanding of the tactics and tools used by hackers. By gaining a thorough understanding of how hackers operate, ethical hackers are able to setup strong countermeasures and defensive systems to protect the organizations critical infrastructure and information.

Books in Series:
- *Ethical Hacking and Countermeasures: Attack Phases*/143548360X
- *Ethical Hacking and Countermeasures: Threats and Defense Mechanisms*/1435483618
- *Ethical Hacking and Countermeasures: Web Applications and Data Servers*/1435483626
- *Ethical Hacking and Countermeasures: Linux, Macintosh and Mobile Systems*/1435483642
- *Ethical Hacking and Countermeasures: Secure Network Infrastructures*/1435483650

Penetration Testing Series

The EC-Council | Press *Penetration Testing* series, preparing learners for E|CSA/LPT certification, is intended for those studying to become Network Server Administrators, Firewall Administrators, Security Testers, System Administrators and Risk Assessment professionals. This series covers a broad base of topics in advanced penetration testing and security analysis. The content of this program is designed to expose the learner to groundbreaking methodologies in conducting thorough security analysis, as well as advanced penetration testing techniques. Armed with the knowledge from the Penetration Testing series, learners will be able to perform the intensive assessments required to effectively identify and mitigate risks to the security of the organization's infrastructure. The series when used in its entirety helps prepare readers to take and succeed on the E|CSA, Certified Security Analyst certification exam.

E|CSA certification is a relevant milestone towards achieving EC-Council's Licensed Penetration Tester (LPT) designation, which also ingrains the learner in the business aspect of penetration testing. To learn more about this designation please visit *http://www.eccouncil.org/lpt.htm*.

Books in Series:
- *Penetration Testing: Security Analysis* /1435483669
- *Penetration Testing: Procedures and Methodologies*/1435483677
- *Penetration Testing: Network and Perimeter Testing* /1435483685
- *Penetration Testing: Communication Media Testing*/1435483693
- *Penetration Testing: Network Threat Testing* /1435483707

Computer Forensics Series

The EC-Council | Press *Computer Forensics* series is intended for those studying to become police investigators and other law enforcement personnel, defense and military personnel, e-business security professionals, systems administrators, legal professionals, banking, insurance and other professionals, government agencies, and IT managers. The content of this program is designed to expose the learner to the process of detecting attacks and collecting evidence in a forensically sound manner with the intent to report crime and prevent future attacks. Advanced techniques in computer investigation and analysis with interest in generating potential legal evidence are included. In full, this series prepares the learner to identify evidence in computer related crime and abuse cases as well as track the intrusive hacker's path through client system.

Books in Series:
- *Computer Forensics: Investigation Procedures and Response*/1435483499
- *Computer Forensics: Investigating Hard Disks, File and Operating Systems*/1435483502
- *Computer Forensics: Investigating Data and Image Files*/1435483510
- *Computer Forensics: Investigating Network Intrusions and Cybercrime*/1435483529
- *Computer Forensics: Investigating Wireless Networks and Devices*/1435483537

Wireless Safety/1435483766

Wireless Safety introduces the learner to the basics of wireless technologies and its practical adaptation. *Wireless Safety* is tailored to cater to any individual's desire to learn more about wireless technology. It requires no prerequisite knowledge and aims to educate the learner in simple applications of these technologies. Topics include wireless signal propagation, IEEE and ETSI Wireless Standards, WLANs and Operation, Wireless Protocols and Communication Languages, Wireless Devices, and Wireless SecurityNetwork. The book also prepares readers to take and succeed on the Wireless|5 certification exam from EC-Council.

Cyber Safety/1435483715

Cyber Safety is designed for anyone who is interested in learning computer networking and security basics. This product provides information cyber crime; security procedures; how to recognize security threats and attacks, incident response, and how to secure internet access. This book gives individuals the basic security literacy skills to begin high-end IT programs. The book also prepares readers to take and succeed on the Security|5 certification exam from EC-Council.

Disaster Recovery Series

The *Disaster Recovery Series* is designed to fortify virtualization technology knowledge of system administrators, systems engineers, enterprise system architects, and any IT professional who is concerned about the integrity of the their network infrastructure. Virtualization technology gives the advantage of additional flexibility as well as cost savings while deploying a disaster recovery solution. The series when used in its entirety helps prepare readers to take and succeed on the E|CDR and E|CVT, Disaster Recovery and Virtualization Technology certification exam from EC-Council. The EC-Council Certified Disaster Recovery and Virtualization Technology professional will have a better understanding of how to setup Disaster Recovery Plans using traditional and virtual technologies to ensure business continuity in the event of a disaster.

Books in Series
- *Disaster Recovery* /1435488709
- *Virtualization Security*/1435488695

Acknowledgements

The Publisher would like acknowledge Jean McKay who served as the subject matter expert reviewer for this book. Jean McKay is the president of PuttyCove, Inc., a firm specializing in project management training/consulting and IT technical instruction.

Jean holds numerous certifications issued by vendors in the IT industry including Microsoft, Cisco, Novell, EC-Council and Comptia, as well as the PMP, and PMP-RMP certifications sponsored by the Project Management Institute. A software developer, a manufacturing firm, and technical training companies formerly employed her as a Senior Trainer, LAN Administrator, and Project Manager.

Planning and leading successful projects to completion, educating team members and other stakeholders in methods to improve their project management skills, and improving processes used on existing projects are among her work. With a focus on risk analysis, disaster recovery, and business continuity, she combines IT expertise with business objectives.

Chapter 1

Foundations of Networks

Objectives

After completing this chapter, you should be able to:

- Understand the basic terminology of networks
- Understand different network models
- Know the types of networks
- Know various network topologies

Key Terms

Client a program or a computer that requests information or resources from another program or computer

Client-server model a dedicated PC or file server has information in one location, where network clients can access files and save them

Local area network (LAN) a network confined to a certain geographic area, such as a single building or a college campus

Mainframe a high-end central computer that can support access to many "dumb" terminals simultaneously

Metropolitan area network (MAN) a group of networks that act together to provide access and services in an area larger than a LAN but not necessarily a WAN; typically locations within one city

Network group of nodes that are connected together using a medium

Network topology the logical and physical arrangement of the computer's interconnection

Peer-to-peer network the resources on one computer can be accessed by any of the peer computers connected to the network

Server a program or computer that provides information or resources to other clients in the network

Wide area network (WAN) unites various LANs that are geographically separate, by using services such as dedicated leased phone lines, dial-up phone lines, satellite links, and data-packet carrier services

Workstation a general-purpose computer that is used to execute applications while connected to a server, from which it accesses data shared by other computers

Case Study

It is the end of the term for Ricky, Wayne, and Desmond, who all major in art. When not studying, they work as freelancers, developing Web-based applications. After the end of every term, they take on small projects, which keep their wallets full. This summer, the trio got a project to build an application that works on a LAN, but they all lived far from each other.

Because Wayne's parents were on vacation, the three decided to work from his home. There was a need for an internal LAN to simulate their application and test it for compatibility issues. So, on a Sunday afternoon, Ricky and Desmond joined Wayne at his place with their respective computers.

Wayne used a broadband connection at home. Ricky brought a hub along with him to set up the internal LAN. Wayne terminated the cable coming from the broadband company to the hub. The individual computers were connected to the hub for Internet access. This was done by connecting their separate LAN ports to the hub using twisted-pair cat 5 with an RJ45 connector. Wayne's IP address was used as the gateway for the other two computers. The DNS used by the two was the same as Wayne's.

After all the hard work, the trio was able to communicate among themselves, as well as surf the Web, without any difficulty.

Introduction to Foundations of Networks

This chapter defines the basic terminology of networks and demonstrates why organizations need them to manage resources, facilitate communication between workgroups, serve clients efficiently, reduce operational costs, and market goods and services productively. Different network models are categorized according to functional relationships; types of networks are discussed according to their range; and four primary network topologies are defined.

What Is a Network?

A *network* is defined as a group of nodes that are connected together using a medium. A node can be a computer, printer, or any peripheral device that is connected to the network. Data is carried over the medium, allowing network nodes to swap documents and data with each other, print with the same printers in the network, and share any hardware or software that is connected to the network. Networks can have any number of nodes.

A network can also be defined as the collection of nodes that process, handle, transfer, and store information, allowing the connection and integration of multiple computers.

The communication medium can be a direct connection, such as networks that are connected using a cable, or an indirect connection, when networks are connected using a modem. The communication medium can be wired or wireless.

The communication between the nodes is managed by using a set of predefined protocols. Within a network, nodes might send information to other nodes that could be on the other side of the world. Networks use addressing mechanisms for data exchange between any two networked nodes. An addressing mechanism is a way of uniquely identifying each node on the network. Similar to a postal address, a house number can only be used once on each street and each street in the town has a different name.

Need for a Network

Groups and organizations rely on networks to manage their resources effectively. If a network connects individuals in an organization, there will be increased employee productivity since information can be shared more effectively. Relevant data reaches intended recipients quickly, saving time, and can be conveniently shared without copying the data to a floppy drive or any physical storage device and carrying it physically to the other person you wish to share the data with. Network users also have access to shared equipment, reducing company expenditures.

Networks can be used by organizations to maintain reliable and up-to-date information from various sources. Ideas can be shared efficiently and decisions can be informed with effective communication between workgroups sharing a network. Being connected can save time, lessening the need for numerous meetings.

Networks can help close communication gaps, allowing organizations to serve their clients more efficiently. With the advent of network proliferation, the cost of communication over the network is greatly reduced. Marketing plans and customer service capabilities are greatly enhanced by the use of networks by employees and clients.

Client, Workstation, and Server

The core components of a network are the clients, workstations, and servers. Each has a specific role in the network and they are all dependent on each other to provide the intended service of the network.

Client

When discussing networks, a *client* is a program or individual computer that requests specific information or resources from another program or computer. Originally, the term *client* referred to computer terminals that could not run programs independently but could communicate with other terminals through a network. In the past, these terminals usually linked as clients sharing time on a mainframe computer.

Workstation

A computer *workstation* is a general-purpose computer that can execute applications while connected to a server, from which it accesses data shared by other computers. A workstation is designed to be used by one person at a time and enables higher performance than most personal computers, such as those intended for home use, in graphics, processing power, and the ability to carry out several tasks at the same time.

Server

A *server* is a program or computer that provides information or resources to other clients in a network. Servers offer software applications that perform tasks for users. These applications include file serving, allowing users to store and access files on a common computer; and application serving, providing software to run programs that carry out tasks for users. Servers can also provide services to the network clients and workstations that are only available from a server-level operating system and are used to help make network access more streamlined and automatic.

Different Network Models

Networks are categorized according to the following parameters: range, functional relationship, network topology, and specialized function. There are three different categories when a network is categorized according to the functional relationship. One category is *peer-to-peer*, when the resources on one computer can be accessed by any of the peer computers connected to the network. Another category is *client-server*. In this model, there is a dedicated PC or file server that stores information in one location. Every client can access the server for files and can save files on the server using a dedicated link provided by the server. This helps in effective management of information. The third category is known as *mainframe*, a high-end central computer that supports access to many "dumb" terminals simultaneously. This is done by sharing the processing time between computers, or operating the processing in batches.

Peer-To-Peer

A *peer-to-peer network* depends on other nodes in the network for computing power, rather than the network itself. In a peer-to-peer network, any node can initiate or finish any transaction of another node. Peer nodes may vary in local configuration, processing speed, and network bandwidth.

For example, consider the peer-to-peer system of e-mail transfer and integrity checking. The sender composes an e-mail. It then travels through many network switches, routers, and mail hubs, and finally reaches the addressee's e-mail account. One method to guarantee the integrity of e-mail is to have all nodes connected along the route know the e-mail protocol and validate the integrity of the e-mail at every step. Changing this system may require including support for HTML e-mails, audio, or video, along with altering the network equipment between each sender and addressee. This would be a huge task. A simpler alternative would have the receiving system notify the sender about a damaged message so the e-mail could be retransmitted.

Some advantages of the peer-to-peer network include affordability and ease of installation. Peer-to-peer networks work well for small offices, where users can manage their own resources and applications.

However, the peer-to-peer network cannot be easily scaled and does not present a safe security solution. It is difficult to categorize and trace information, because all data is uniformly distributed between networked computers. All users could potentially be affected if a computer in the network crashes.

Client-Server

In order to make use of the services available on this type of network, application programs that run on separate computers must communicate efficiently. In other words, the application programs are the entities that communicate with each other, not the computers.

The application programs follow the *client-server model* to communicate with each other. An application program, running on one of the computers called *client*, solicits for a service from another application program, called *server*. The server application program provides services for any client in the network. The relationship between clients and server is many-to-one. The server program should always be running in order to provide the required services for the clients. In contrast, the client program is run only when it requires a service.

Advantages of the client-server model include centralized services, where the server manages resources and data security; scalability, with single or multiple elements able to be replaced separately as needed; and flexibility, with new technology easily incorporated into the scheme. Other advantages feature interoperability, with all modules (client, server, and workstations) working together, and accessibility of a server that can be accessed remotely and across diverse platforms.

However, the required hardware and software for this network type is very expensive, and the system is only efficient for large networks of users.

Mainframe

A mainframe is a high-end central computer that can support access to many terminals simultaneously. Mainframes can support multiple users simultaneously, who access through "dumb" terminals. The mainframe then supports the terminals by sharing time or operating in batches, where users do not have direct computing power. Mainframes were originally named because of their large size and requirement of specialized HVAC and electrical power. At the present time, mainframes support access through any user interface, including the Internet.

A few mainframes have the capability to run multiple operating systems, and operate as a number of "virtual machines," instead of a single computer. A single mainframe can substitute for many smaller servers, reducing management and administrative costs by improving scalability and reliability. The reliability is enhanced because of hardware redundancy, and the scalability is accomplished because of the relocation of hardware resources among the "virtual machines" as needed. The cost advantage of doing this is usually negated by the high cost of the mainframe. Most mid- to high-end servers now have this high-availability feature that was previously only available on mainframes.

The advantages of a mainframe include high reliability, proven technology, raw computing power, business-critical applications, and large storage infrastructures.

However, mainframes require a high preliminary expenditure and may have inadequate software/support. Also, a centralized computer can be a disadvantage; when the mainframe is down, the entire network goes down. See Figure 1-1 to examine a mainframe network configuration.

Types of Networks

Networks are categorized by range; there are three primary categories. See Figure 1-2 for a network category breakdown.

Local Area Network (LAN)

A *local area network (LAN)* is a network confined to a certain geographic area, such as a single building or a college campus. LANs can be of any size, connecting several computers or linking hundreds of computers used by thousands of people. Improvement in standard networking protocols and media has caused the proliferation of LANs all over businesses and educational organizations.

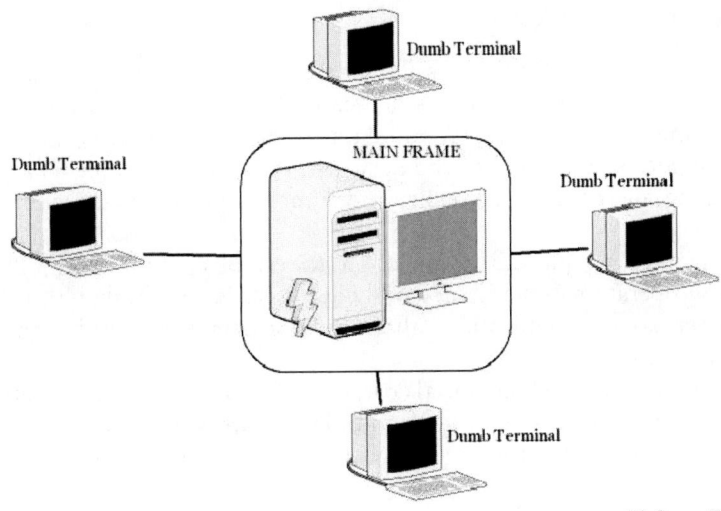

Figure 1-1 A mainframe network configuration.

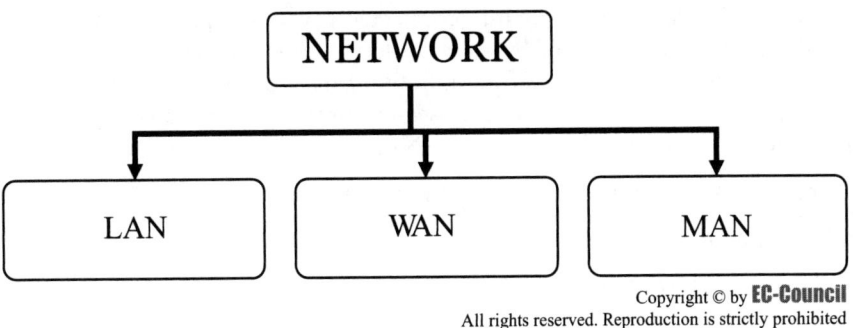

Figure 1-2 Network categories.

The typical characteristics of LANs are:
- Inexpensive medium of data transmission
- Multiple computers connected to shared medium
- High total bandwidth (~10–100 Mb/s)
- Low delay
- Low error rate
- Broadcast/multicast capability
- Limited geography (1–2 km)
- Limited number of workstations
- Peer relationship between stations

Some advantages of a LAN include:
- Highly reliable network (computers do not rely on each other).
- Easily scalable, high data transmission rate.
- Other computers can share peripheral devices.

The failure of the communication medium will lead to an entire network system breakdown.

Wide Area Network (WAN)

A *wide area network (WAN)* unites various LANs that are geographically separate. This can be done by linking different LANs using services such as dedicated leased phone lines, dial-up phone lines (both synchronous and asynchronous), satellite links, and data-packet carrier services. A WAN's complexity depends on the number of computers connected to the network. It can be as simple as a dial-up network, or it may require complex routing algorithms, protocols, and filters to minimize the expenditure on other means of communication.

WANs typically require no physical connection to establish a network, transmit through telephone and satellite links, can operate nationally or worldwide, have lesser bandwidth (~1800–9600 bps), can overcome time lags in overseas communication, allow remote data entry, and require centralized information maintenance.

Although WANs have a relatively high initial cost, there is usually low augmentation cost per connection and they support multicasting. Multicasting allows multiple recipients to receive messages without overwhelming the network, which would happen if the message were sent to all hosts. The message is sent only to a specific list of hosts.

Metropolitan Area Network (MAN)

A *metropolitan area network (MAN)* is a group of networks that act together to provide access and services in an area larger than a LAN but not necessarily a WAN; typically, locations are within one city. A MAN is a single, unique, exclusive "Metro Area Network" that is owned and managed by a single network operator, service provider, or carrier. It selects data from interconnected LANs and passes it to another LAN or WAN in the same geographical area. LANs are defined by their borders; the "enterprise edge" where the network ends. But a MAN is portrayed in terms of distance and function. In terms of distance, a MAN covers up to 150 kilometers. In terms of function, the use of a MAN is to offer secure distributed broadband access to users.

The typical characteristics of a MAN include LANs interconnected across a metropolitan area:

- Sharing of resources and connection to other networks
- Large-scale private phone service
- High-speed service (~100's Mb/s)
- Coverage up to 150 km
- High-performance cable and equipment

An example of a MAN is an Ethernet network, which uses coaxial or fiber-optic cable for data transmission; a protocol called Carrier Sense Multiple Access with Collision Detection (CSMA/CD) is used by the components to access the network.

Various Network Topologies

Network topology is defined as the logical and physical arrangement of the computer interconnection. There are four primary network topology categories. They are ring, mesh, star, and bus.

Ring Topology

In a ring topology, devices are linked in a closed loop. Because there are no unconnected ends, no terminators are required. A signal is passed along the ring in one direction, from one device to the next, until it reaches its destination.

The advantages of a ring topology include easy reconfiguration and installation, ease of expansion, and simplified fault isolation. If one device does not receive a signal, it can issue an alarm.

A ring topology's disadvantages result from unidirectional traffic, and a break in the ring can disable the entire network. See Figure 1-3 for a representation of a ring topology.

Mesh Topology

In the mesh topology, devices are connected with many redundant interconnections between network nodes. This is the preferable topology for WANs. Mesh topologies exploit routers to determine the best path; there is a dedicated point-to-point connection to every node in the network.

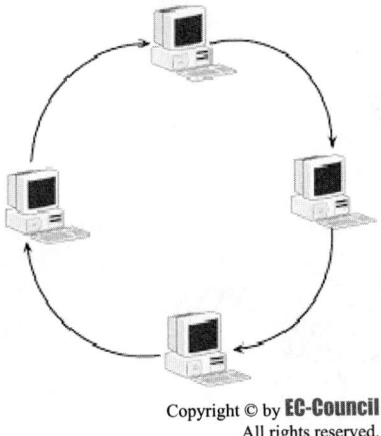

Figure 1-3 Devices linked in a ring topology.

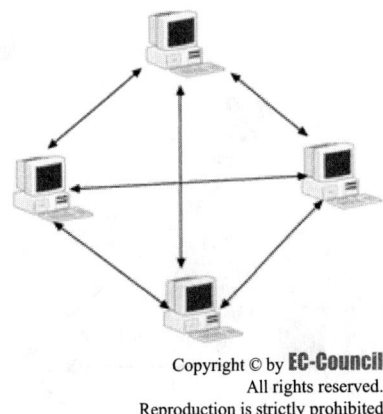

Figure 1-4 Representation of a mesh topology.

Mesh topologies eliminate traffic problem as each connection carries its own data load. They are robust and make fault detection and fault isolation easier. But, more cabling is required, installation and reconfiguration is difficult, and they are expensive because of the hardware needed to connect each link. See Figure 1-4 for the configuration of a mesh topology.

Star Topology

In a star topology, all devices such as file servers, workstations, and peripherals are directly connected to a central network hub or concentrator. These devices are not directly linked to each other. If one device wants to send data to another, it sends the data to the controller, which then relays data to another connected device.

In star topologies, installation and reconfiguring is easy. They are robust; if one link fails, all other links remain active. These topologies provide easy fault detection and fault isolation, so there are no disruptions to the network when connecting or removing devices.

However, more cabling is required than in a bus. Also, if the central network hub or concentrator fails, all linked nodes are disabled. Finally, they are more expensive because of the use of a concentrator. See Figure 1-5 for an example of a star topology.

Tree Bus Topology

A tree bus topology arranges nodes in the network that resemble a tree. This results in an interconnection of star networks; individual peripheral nodes, or "leaves," can transmit to and receive from other nodes, and are not required to act as repeaters or regenerators. But unlike the star network, the function of the central node may be distributed.

The nodes in the tree bus topology are connected to a central hub, called the *active hub*, which controls the network traffic. The secondary hub, called the *passive hub*, provides a physical connection between the network components.

The tree bus topology is easily scalable, and can isolate and prioritize communications from different computers. See Figure 1-6 for a representation of a tree bus topology.

Linear Bus Topology

The linear bus topology is multipoint. It is a linear configuration, where one long cable acts as a backbone to all the devices in the network. Nodes are connected to the linear bus topology by drop lines and taps. A drop line is a connection running between the device and the main cable. A tap is a connector that links in to the main cable to make contact with the metallic core.

The linear bus topology is easy to install, with less cabling required than other topologies. However, reconfiguration, fault isolation, and expansion are difficult, and the entire network shuts down if there is a break in the main cable. This topology is not suitable to be used as a standalone solution in a large building.

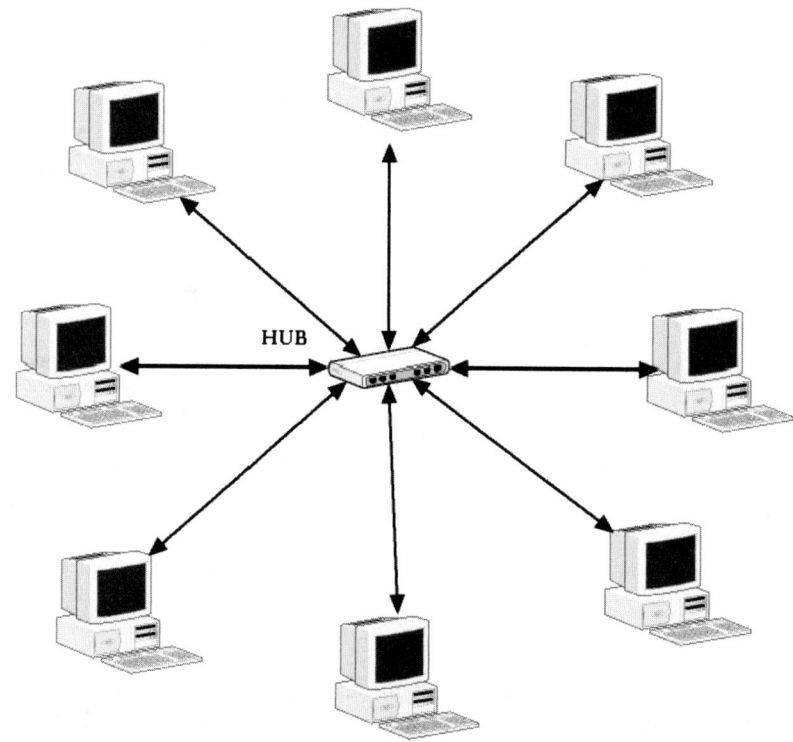

Figure 1-5 A star topology configuration.

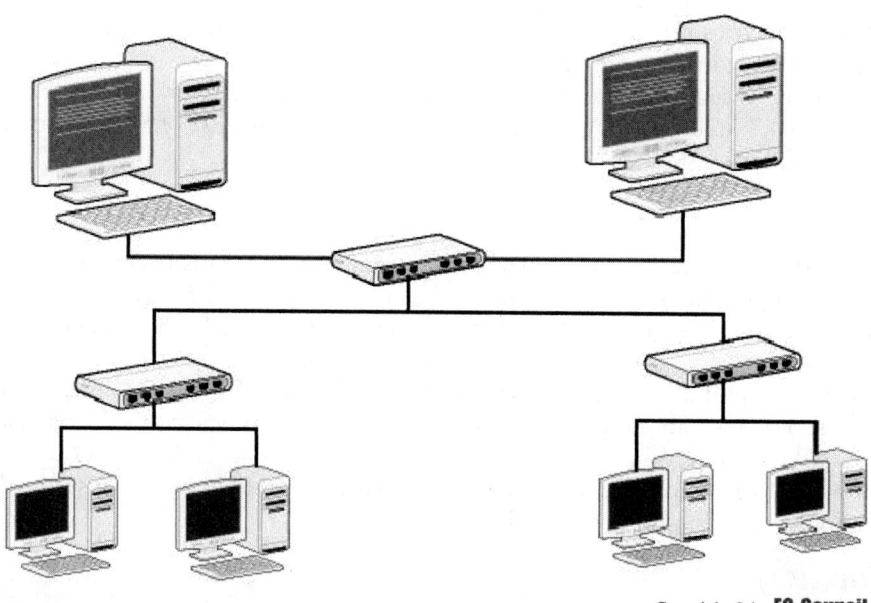

Figure 1-6 Configuration of a tree bus topology.

Chapter Summary

- A network is defined as a set of computers and peripherals connected together using a medium.
- Networks are needed to manage resources, update information, share files, and assist the expansion of business marketing efforts.
- Different network models are the peer-to-peer model, the client-server model and mainframes.
- The primary types of networks are LAN, WAN, and MAN.
- Types of network topologies include ring, mesh, star, and the bus variations.

Review Questions

1. What is a node, with reference to computer networks?

2. Give four reasons why groups and organizations rely on networks.

3. What is the relationship between a client and a server on a network?

4. List three different categories of network models, and the similarities/differences of each.

5. What are the primary categories of types of networks, when classified by geographic range?

6. What are the advantages of each type of network?

7. What are network topologies?

8. How are network nodes connected in a ring topology? A mesh topology? A star topology? Tree bus and linear bus topologies?

9. What are the advantages of each topology?

10. Which topologies provide easy fault detection and fault isolation?

Hands-On Projects

1. Determine which network model is followed by your classroom network.
2. Determine the network topology used in your classroom network.
3. Find out the geographic limit of your classroom's network.
4. Try connecting computers in a ring topology.
5. Reconfigure your classroom's network, and try connecting the computers in a mesh topology. What is the difference?

Chapter 2

Network Components

Objectives

After completing this chapter, you should be able to:
- Understand network components
- Understand the types of network cables
- Know the media connectors
- Know how to choose a cable

Key Terms

Bridges   devices designed to connect different LANs, or two segments of the same LAN

Brouters   a single protocol or multiprotocol router that acts as either a router or a bridge

Coaxial cable   cable that has a solid core surrounded by tubular conductor (braid, foil, or both); the entire assembly is covered with an insulating and protective layer

Fiber-optic cable   cable that converts electrical signal to optical signal, transmits the optical signal, and reconverts it to electrical signal

Gateways   device that connects networks with different communication protocols, or architectures, and translates between the networks

Hubs   network hardware that is used for connecting segments of a LAN

Repeaters   a device used in a bus topology to expand maximum distance that can be covered in a cable run

Routers   devices that transfer data packets along networks

Shielded twisted-pair (STP) cable   cable that has an outer covering, which is braided casting identical to coaxial cable, and provides the best protection from interference

Switches   central components of networks that interconnect computers in LANs and route information from one network type to another

Unshielded twisted-pair (UTP) cable   the basic type of wire that is used for telecommunications, and commonly used for computer networking; does not have an outer covering

USB (Universal Serial Bus)   an interface for slow-speed peripherals

Introduction to Network Components

This chapter will introduce common components necessary when setting up different network infrastructures. Different types of network components and cables will be discussed, and various media connectors will be defined. This chapter will also outline how to choose the proper cable for specific networking scenarios.

Network Components

Today, there are a large number of products to consider when setting up your network infrastructure. There are devices available for everything, from connecting computers to a network to controlling network traffic.

Some products, however, require extensive planning before selection. For example, you have to decide whether your network needs a bridge, a switch, or a router to control network traffic. People tend to buy hardware according to the vendor's recommendations, which may prove futile. Each device has its own unique characteristics and has been manufactured with a certain purpose in mind. The purpose must be an exact match for the manner in which the user is going to handle the network. This section will define and discuss some of the common network components used.

Repeaters

As simple two-port signal amplifiers, *repeaters* are devices used in a bus topology to expand the maximum distance that can be covered in a cable run (Figure 2-1). The strength of the signal is boosted as it travels down the wire. A repeater will receive a digital signal on one of its ports, amplify it, and transmit it out of another port. A repeater does not distinguish data quality; it simply looks at each of the individual digital pulses and amplifies them. A repeater is a cheap, effective way of extending your cable lengths.

Hubs

Hubs are network hardware that are used for connecting segments of a LAN (Figure 2-2). They are probably the most common piece of network hardware, except network interface cards. Hubs serve as a common connection point for all devices present in a network. Physically, they are boxes of varying sizes that have multiple female RJ-45 connectors. Each connector is designed to accept one twisted-pair cable outfitted with a male RJ-45 connector.

Figure 2-1 A repeater is a simple two-port amplifier.

Figure 2-2 Hubs are probably the most common piece of network hardware.

Bridges

A *bridge* is a device designed to connect different LANs, or two segments of the same LAN (Figure 2-3). It looks like a small box with two network connectors that connect to two separate portions of a network. A bridge integrates the functionality of a repeater (signal amplification), but it looks at the outline of data, which is a great benefit. A common bridge is nearly indistinguishable from a repeater, except for the indicator lights. A forward light flashes whenever a bridge relays transmitting traffic from one collision domain to another.

Bridges make use of frame header information by observing the source and destination MAC address on each frame of data. By assessing the source, the bridge will gain knowledge about where all the network systems are situated. It will create a table, listing which MAC addresses are directly reachable by each of its ports. It will then use that data to function as a traffic cop, and standardize the flow of data on a network.

Routers

Routers are devices or software that transfer data packets along networks (Figure 2-4). They are connected to at least two networks, either two LANs, WANs, or a LAN and its ISP network. Routers are located at gateways, the devices used to connect the access point, the Internet, and a wired network.

A router can be a simple hardware device that can execute specific tasks just like a switch, a central component of networks that interconnect computers in LANs and route information from one network type to another. However, some routers are more sophisticated. They have access to network-layer addresses, and contain software that enables them to determine which of several possible paths between those addresses is most suitable for a particular transmission. Routers use header and forwarding tables to determine the best path for forwarding data packets. They use protocols, such as ICMP, to communicate with each other and configure the best route between any two hosts.

A router can also be software in a computer that determines the next network point to which a data packet has to be sent en route to its destination. It decides which way the data packet should be sent, based on its current knowledge of the network it is connected to. Routers are located at any point where one network meets another. A router creates and maintains a table of all the routes available, their conditions, and the cost of the route. This table is known as the routing table. The routing function is associated with the network layer of the OSI model.

Figure 2-3 A bridge looks similar to a repeater.

Figure 2-4 A router can be a simple hardware device or a software program.

Figure 2-5 Switches look like stackable hubs.

Switches

Switches are the central components of networks that interconnect computers in LANs and route information from one network type to another (Figure 2-5). They represent a combination of hub and bridge technologies. Switches are an essential part of numerous networks because they are fast. Switches permit different nodes in a network to communicate directly with each other in a smooth and resourceful manner.

They look like stackable hubs in appearance, having multiple RJ-45 connectors for linking network systems. But, instead of being dumb amplifiers like hubs, switches operate as little miniature bridges built into each port. A switch will keep track of MAC addresses attached to each port and route traffic meant for a specific address to the appropriate port.

Gateways

A *gateway* connects networks with different communication protocols, or architectures, and translates between the networks. Gateways are intelligent devices; normally, they function on the transport layer, and on session, presentation, and application layers.

A gateway is used as a protocol convertor. It can accept a packet formatted for one protocol and convert it to a packet formatted for another protocol before forwarding it. A gateway is usually software installed within a router. The gateway understands the protocols used by each network linked into the router, and is able to translate from one protocol to another. In some cases, the only modifications necessary are the header and trailer of the packet. In other cases, the gateway must adjust the data rate, size, and format.

Brouters

A *brouter* is a combination of a bridge and a router (Figure 2-6). It is a single protocol or multiprotocol router that acts as either a router or a bridge. A brouter checks incoming data packets first to decide whether they are from a routable protocol. For example, protocols such as TCP/IP can be routed, but Microsoft's NetBEUI protocol cannot be routed.

If the brouter determines the data packet is routable, it uses its routing tables just as a router would, to determine where to route the packet. If, on the other hand, the packet is from a nonroutable protocol, the brouter looks at the MAC address stored within the frames being sent and uses its bridging tables to determine the proper recipient.

Types of Networking Cables

There are four common types of cables used for computer networking that vary according to prescribed use, appearance, vulnerability, and data transfer rate:

1. The *unshielded twisted-pair (UTP)* cable is a basic type of wire that is used for telecommunications, and is commonly used for wired computer networking. It does not have an outer covering.
2. The *shielded twisted-pair (STP)* cable has an outer covering, which is braided casting identical to coaxial cable, and provides the best protection from interference. It is not vulnerable to electrical or radio-frequency interference.
3. *Coaxial cable* has a solid core surrounded by tubular conductor (braid, foil, or both); the entire assembly is covered with an insulating and protective layer. This cable is highly guarded from interference.
4. Finally, *fiber-optic cable* converts electrical signal to optical signal, transmits the optical signal, and reconverts it to electrical signal. It has a high data-transfer rate.

Figure 2-6 Brouters are a combination of bridges and routers.

Media Connectors

In a wired environment, it is necessary to connect various media sources, such as telephones, video monitors, computer mice, modems, and keyboards, into computing devices. Media connectors attach to specific media transmitting data, and allow a physical connection to another peripheral. This section will identify different connectors associated with specifc media.

RJ-11 (Registered Jack)

The RJ-11 is a standard telephone line connector used in telephone modular cords between the wall and telephone (Figure 2-7). It is also used to connect computers in a PCnet-Home network. This connector has up to six pins and the width of the plastic housing is approximately three-eighths inch.

RJ-45 (Registered Jack)

The RJ-45 is used with Ethernet twisted-pair links (Figure 2-8). It is commonly used in 10Base-T, 100Base-TX, 100Base-T2, and 1000Base-T physical-layer types. An RJ-45 connector has eight pins and is known as an 8-pin modular connector. A male RJ-45 plug is placed on each end of the twisted-pair cable; the female RJ-45 jack is built into the Ethernet hub or NIC.

IEEE 1394

The IEEE 1394 is an international bus standard that supports data transfer rates of up to 400 Mbps (in 1394) and 800 Mbps (in 1394b). It provides a plug-and-play-compatible expansion interface for the computer that can be used to connect up to 63 external devices (Figure 2-9). This connector can transfer high levels of data in real time, making it ideal for audio/video (A/V) appliances, storage peripherals, and portable devices. The IEEE 1394 has self-configured addressing, eliminating address conflicts; users do not have to set address switches.

USB

The *USB (Universal Serial Bus)* is an interface for slow-speed peripherals (Figure 2-10). This connector is a computer standard designed to support data transfer rates of 12 Mbps. It removes the guesswork in linking peripherals to a computer by providing connectivity for up to 127 peripheral devices, such as mice, modems, and keyboards. The USB also supports installations of plug-and-play and hot plugging.

How to Choose a Cable

Deciding which type of cable to use when setting up a network depends on the number of computers to be linked together and the length of the network.

Use 10BaseT cabling for 16 or fewer PCs within a 325-foot radius of each other. Portable computers would also call for 10BaseT cable.

Use thin coax cabling for fewer than 10 PCs in a network that will include no portable computers.

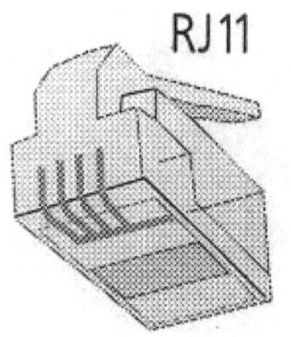

Figure 2-7 An RJ-11 standard telephone line connector.

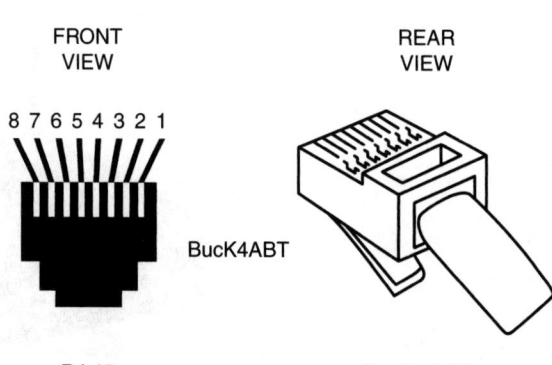

Figure 2-8 The RJ-45 jack is known as an 8-pin modular connector.

Figure 2-9 An IEEE 1394 connector can connect up to 63 external devices.

Figure 2-10 USB connectors provide connectivity to peripheral devices such as mice, modems, and keyboards.

Chapter Summary

- Each network component has its own unique characteristics and has been manufactured with a certain purpose in mind.
- The needs of the network must match how the user is going to implement the network.
- There are seven common network components to consider when setting up a network.

- A repeater is an inexpensive and effective way of extending cable lengths.
- Hubs serve as common connection points for all devices present in a network.
- A bridge is a small box with two network connectors that connect to two separate portions of a network.
- A router is located where two or more networks connect, and can also be software in a computer that determines the next point to which a packet has to be sent en route to its destination.
- Switches are a combination of hub and bridge technologies. A brouter is a single protocol or multiprotocol router that acts as either a router or a bridge.
- Media connectors transmit data by allowing a physical connection to another peripheral, and there are four common connectors: RJ-11, RJ-45, IEEE 1394, and USB.
- Choosing the proper cable when setting up networks depends on distance and the number of computers to be included.

Review Questions

1. What does a repeater allow with regard to distance in a cable run?

2. What purpose do hubs serve in a network?

3. Which network component would allow different LANs to be connected?

4. Where are routers located in a network configuragion?

5. Which network technologies do switches combine?

6. What purpose does a gateway serve in a network, and where is this software installed?

7. What two network component functions are combined in a brouter?

8. How do media connectors function in a network?

9. How do you choose a cable type when setting up a network?

10. What are the four most common networking cables available?

Hands-On Projects

1. Identify the components used in your classroom network.
2. Locate the type of network cable used in your classroom and list its characteristics.
3. Determine the types of media connectors used to link peripherals to your PC.

Chapter 3

LAN Technologies

Objectives

After completing this chapter, you should be able to:

- Understand Ethernet and its characteristics
- List the different categories of Ethernet
- List Ethernet cable types
- Understand a virtual private network (VPN)
- Understand how to connect to a VPN using Windows 2000

Key Terms

10Base2   in IEEE 802.3 implementation of the Ethernet, the second standard that is defined is thin Ethernet, or Thinnet

10Base5   the first standard defined by the IEEE 802.3 model, also called thick Ethernet, or Thicknet

10BaseT   in IEEE 802.3 implementation of the Ethernet, this is the third and most popular standard; also known as twisted-pair Ethernet

10Broad36   the only broadband Ethernet standard that uses a coaxial cable for transmission

Attachment unit interface (AUI)   a connector on an Ethernet card that is used in connecting various coaxial, fiber-optic, or twisted-pair cable

Baseband   "base" denotes digital signal

Broadband   "broad" denotes analog signal

Carrier Sense Multiple Access with Collision Detection (CSMA/CD)   protocol used by the components to share a network

CATV   cabling that is an acronym for Community Antenna Television; it is coaxial cabling used for transmission of cable TV signals, but is also used with Ethernet 10Broad36 networks.

Ethernet   an arbitration mechanism used to resolve conflicts when two or more computers in a network transmit data simultaneously

Fast Ethernet   a networking standard that supports data transfer rates up to 100 Mbps by decreasing the collision domain, the maximum distance data travels between two stations on a network

Gigabit Ethernet   operates at 1,000 Mb/s by reducing the collision domain

Multimode Fiber (MMF)   this cable allows multiple lights to propagate through the fiber optic; a large core allows coupling from cheaper LEDs, couplers, and connectors

Network Interface Cards   cards that have the circuitry to help stations get connected to networks

Single-Mode Fiber (SMF)   cable that transmits data from a single, small, expensive light source

Switched Ethernet   an enhanced version of the 10Base5 standard Ethernet model, in which the hub in the star topology is replaced by a switch, which recognizes the destination address and transmits data to its respective destination, rather than broadcasting packets of data to all computers in the network

Thicknet   also known as thick Ethernet, 10-mm-thick coaxial cable used for the IEEE standard Ethernet 10Base5 networks

Thinnet   uses 5-mm coaxial cable that is an inexpensive alternative for Thicknet; used for the IEEE standard Ethernet 10Base2 networks

Transreceiver   a device that receives and transmits the signal

Twinax   also called twin axial, one of the types of coaxial cable

Virtual private network (VPN)   a private network that is used in an organization, or by a group of organizations, to include, summarize, encrypt, and validate links across a shared or public network

Case Study

Scarlet has decided to set up a LAN in her home so that she and brother Joe can share the same Internet connection and resources. Joe is in his final year of school and is working on a project under the guidance of Scarlet.

Scarlet has a problem. She is not sure which cable needs to be used for establishing connectivity between the two computers and whether to use a hub or a switch. Scarlet is also planning to connect one more computer, which will be used as a backup, so she needs to determine the network topology to be used when she connects the three computers.

Can you help Scarlet in clearing up her doubts? Which type of cable would be best to connect the computers? What network topology would best suit her needs?

Introduction to LAN Technologies

This chapter defines and describes the different types of Ethernet networking technologies. Various Ethernet cable types are discussed, the characteristics of virtual private networks (VPNs) are presented, and VPN connectivity using Windows 2000 is illustrated.

Ethernet and Its Characteristics

Ethernet is an arbitration mechanism used to resolve conflicts when two or more computers in a network transmit data simultaneously. It is a LAN standard and technically known as IEEE 802.3. With proper network software and hardware, any computer can use Ethernet. Computers with different operating systems and peripherals can communicate with each other using this common protocol. This standard is named after luminiferous Ether, through which electromagnetic radiation was once thought to propagate.

When a station wants to transmit data, it listens to the cable; if the cable is busy, the station waits for the cable to become idle. When two or more data packets collide, the station waits for a random amount of time and retransmits the data.

Ethernet is defined only in the data-link and physical layers of the Open Systems Interconnect (OSI) reference model. The combination of software (Ethernet card driver) and hardware (Ethernet card/controller chip) controls the data transmitted to a network and the acceptance of it. Software is responsible for the destination address, source address, and data.

Ethernet has become popular, because it achieves a fine balance between speed, cost, and ease of installation. When these benefits are combined with mass approval in the computer market and the capability to cooperate with almost all network protocols, Ethernet provides an ideal networking technology.

Physical Characteristics

The physical characteristics of Ethernet include a distance range of 2.5 meters to 2.5 kilometers. Cable used for this network depends on the network's characteristics; coaxial, twisted-pair, or fiber-optic cable can be used. *Carrier Sense Multiple Access with Collision Detection (CSMA/CD)* is a protocol used by components to share a network. CSMA/CD regulates the network traffic.

Other physical characteristics include data packets, in which data is transmitted in variable-length frames that contain destination and source address, control information, and up to 1,500 bytes of data. The Ethernet's speed offers baseband transmission at 10 megabits per second.

The hardware interface consists of two components. The *transreceiver*, a device that receives and transmits the signal, is a component that only involves sending and receiving frames, and detecting collisions. It is electrically secluded from the host computer and synchronizes its bit-rate clock with data frames. The *network interface* includes hardware that defines the network address of the connection. It verifies the address of all frames and rejects those that do not have proper addresses, retransmits all frames that are damaged due to collisions, and forwards the received frames to their respective destinations.

Different Categories in Ethernet

Ethernet type is mainly defined by the type of signal transmitted, the speed of transmission, and the type of cable and its length. There are two categories of Ethernet: *baseband*, in which "base" denotes digital signal; and *broadband*, in which "broad" denotes digital signal. These categories are summarized in Table 3-1.

Standard	Data Rate	Topology	Medium	Max. Seg. Length
10Base5	10 Mb/s	Bus	Thick Ethernet	500 m
10Base2	10 Mb/s	Bus	Thin Ethernet	200 m
10Base-T	10 Mb/s	Star	Twisted pair	100 m
1Base5	1 Mb/s	Star	Twisted telephone cable	250 m
100Base-T	100 Mb/s	Star	UTP cable	100 m
10Base36	10 Mb/s	Bus	Broadband cable	180 m

Table 3-1 Comparison of the IEEE 802.3 model standards in baseband and broadband

A representation of Ethernet type can be explained as follows:

Where X is a number and represents the speed of the data transmission in Mb/s., base/broad represents the type of signal Y, a number or a letter, which represents type of cable used and its length (Figure 3-1).

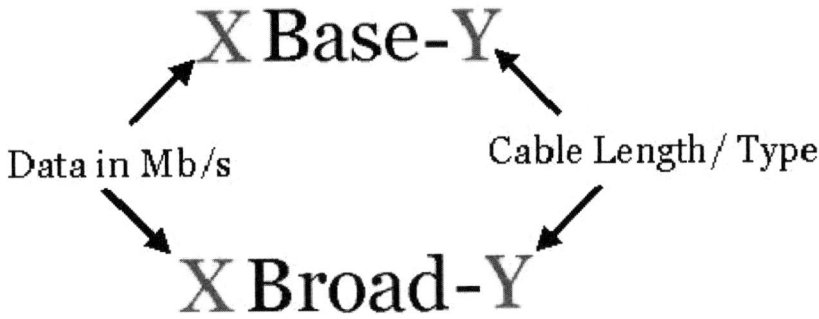

Figure 3-1 Ethernet types.

Baseband Ethernet

The IEEE 802.3 model, a collection of standards that specify the technology for wired Ethernet, indicates five standards for baseband Ethernet. This section will define three of these baseband standards.

10Base5

10Base5 is the first standard defined by the IEEE 802.3 model. It is also called thick Ethernet or **Thicknet** because the 10-mm-thick coaxial cable is heavy and inflexible (Figure 3-2). The maximum length of the segment is 500 meters, and baseband signaling is used for the signal transmission. The 10Base5 is a bus topology.

To overcome the size limitation of LANs, networking devices such as repeaters and bridges are used. In thick Ethernet, each segment has a restricted length of 500 meters. In order to reduce the number of collisions, a maximum of five segments can be used. Also, each station must be separated by at least 2.5 meters.

Various physical connectors and cables are utilized, which include coaxial cable; **network interface cards**, which have the circuitry to help stations get connected with networks; transreceivers; and an **attachment unit interface (AUI)**, a connector on an Ethernet card that is used in connecting various cables.

Thicknet is very reliable if the network is installed and configured properly. Also, nodes can be easily added by tapping into existing cable segments. However, installation of the thick, heavy, and inflexible cable is a challenge, isolating problems is difficult in bus topology, and high-speed Ethernet standards are not compatible with a coaxial medium.

10Base2

Also known as thin Ethernet or **Thinnet**, which uses a 5-mm coaxial cable that is an inexpensive alternative for Thicknet, *10Base2* is the second standard in the IEEE 802.3 implementation of Ethernet. While serving as an economical substitute for the 10Base5 Ethernet, the data rate in 10Base2 is similar. 10Base2 is a bus topology LAN, and is easy to install. In thin Ethernet, each segment has a restricted length of 185 meters and up to six segments may be used. In order to reduce number of collisions, nodes per segment must not exceed 30.

Various physical connectors and cables are utilized, which include thin coaxial cable, network interface cards, and BNC-T connectors. Figure 3-3 shows a Thinnet configuration.

Thinnet's advantages include a comparatively easier installation than Thicknet because of the thinner cables, and reduced expenditure for the network by eliminating the external transreceiver. However, Thinnet is unreliable and it is difficult to troubleshoot the chained segments. Also, chained segments are not compatible for office environments, and high-speed Ethernet standards are not compatible with a coaxial medium.

10BaseT

In the IEEE 802.3 implementation of Ethernet, the third and the most popular standard defined is twisted-pair Ethernet or *10BaseT*. Twisted-pair Ethernet is a star topology LAN that uses unshielded twisted-pair (UTP)

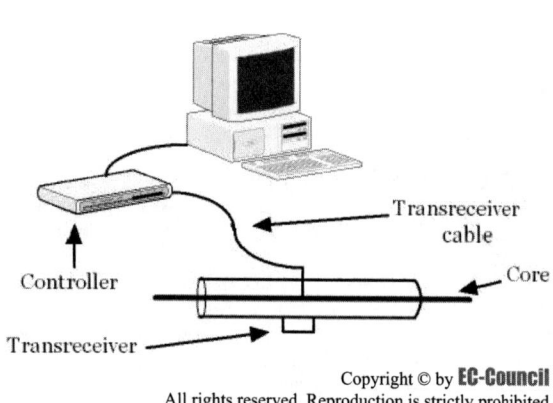

Figure 3-2 Thicknet uses inflexible cable.

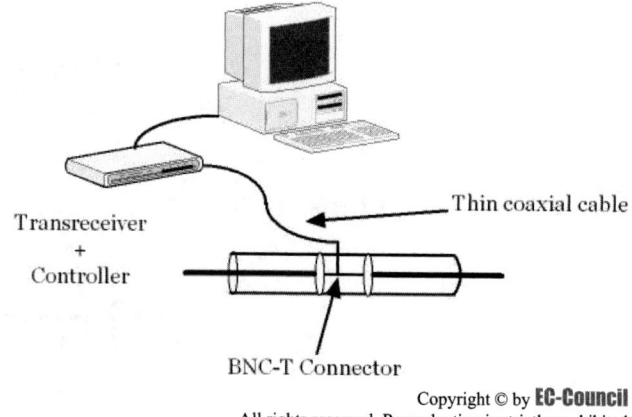

Figure 3-3 A Thinnet network configuration.

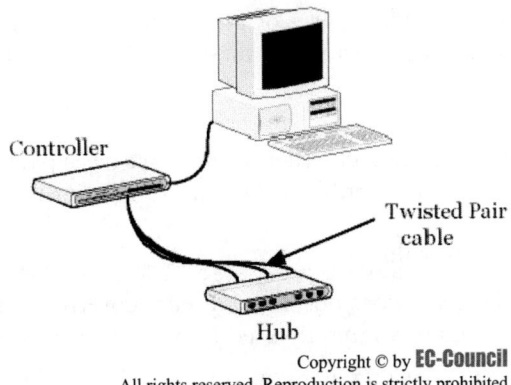

Figure 3-4 A twisted-pair Ethernet configuration.

cable instead of coaxial cable (Figure 3-4). This LAN supports a data rate of 10 Mbps; the maximum length of cable between the hub and the station cannot exceed 100 meters.

Unlike the other IEEE 802.3 standards, 10Base-T uses an intelligent hub with a port for each station. Stations are linked into the hub using an RJ45 connector. In twisted-pair Ethernet, each segment has a restricted length of 100 meters. In order to reduce the number of collisions, nodes per segment must not exceed 1,024.

Various physical connectors and cables are utilized in 10BaseT, which include UTP cables, a hub, network interface cards, and an RJ-45 connector.

The star topology used in 10BaseT helps is easy to maintain and troubleshoot. Also, UTP cable is inexpensive and widely used.

Broadband Ethernet

Broadband technology allows for high-speed connections to the Internet. This section will detail 10Broad36, the only broadband Ethernet standard that uses a coaxial cable for transmission.

10Broad36

10Broad36 is an Ethernet standard, using inexpensive coaxial cable identical to the cable used in cable television. This cable can support transmission of multiple services to multiple users on the same cable by sharing the bandwidth at different frequencies; every frequency is allocated to a different service. This technique allows 10Broad36 to share a single cable with other services.

In baseband transmission (10Base5 and 10Base2), the signal flow is bidirectional; with broadband transmission, the signal flow is unidirectional, traveling in only one direction along the cable. For the signal to arrive at all the components in a network, a data flow path must be created. This can be achieved by configuring the network using a "single cable" or "dual cable" configuration.

In a single cable configuration, the cable transmits on two channels, with each channel having a different frequency range. One channel at a particular frequency carries signals, and the other channel receives the signals.

In a dual cable configuration, every station is connected with a pair of cables. One cable always transmits the signal to the destination, and the other cable always receives the signal.

10Broad36 supports much longer segment lengths than 10Base5 and 10Base2, allowing for a maximum distance of 1,800 meters between two stations. However, this standard is not capable of supporting the full-duplex mode of operation. Full duplex uses two pairs of wires at the same time instead of one, as in half duplex. Data transfer is faster, and there are no collisions.

Ethernet Cable Types

Ethernet cables are categorized into three types. Twisted-pair cables contain two insulated copper wires twisted together to cancel out electromagnetic interference known as cross talk. The number of twists per meter makes up part of the specification for a given type of cable. The greater the number of twists, the more cross talk is reduced.

Coaxial cable consists of a round conducting wire, which is surrounded by an insulating spacer; the next layer is a cylindrical conducting sheath, usually surrounded by a final insulating layer.

Fiber-optic cable uses a technology in which glass or plastic threads transmit data. These cables consist of a bundle of glass threads; each is capable of transmitting messages that modulate into light waves.

Twisted-Pair Cable

This cable has pairs of wires twisted around each other. Every cable has a pair of insulated copper wires twisted together to reduce cross talk and noise susceptibility. Quality of the twisted pairs depends on the number of twists per inch.

There are three types of twisted-pair cable.

- Unshielded twisted-pair cable (UTP) does not have an outer covering. It is the basic type of wire that is used for telecommunications, and is commonly used for computer networking.
- Shielded twisted-pair cable (STP) has an outer covering, which is braided identical to coaxial cable, and presents the best protection from interference. It consists of four-pair UTP cable, with a single foil separating all four pairs; this decreases radiation and vulnerability to outside noise.
- Screened twisted-pair cable, or Foil twisted-pair (FTP), is a four-pair UTP cable with the twisted pairs individually wrapped in a foil shield and surrounded by an outer braided wire shield.

Twisted-pair cables can block unwanted interference, lower data loss at high frequencies per unit length, and easily establish connection. However, twisted-pair cable is more vulnerable to electrical interference from other electric cables and systems, making transmission slow.

Coaxial Cable

Coaxial cable has a solid center wire called a *conductor*. The solid center is usually made of copper and wrapped by insulating foam. The insulation is enclosed by foil or wire, and then covered in a plastic sheath. Electrical signals, or data, use the solid center conductor as a path on the network. An example of coaxial, or coax, cabling is cable TV, which uses this type of connection for carrying data, voice, and video simultaneously.

There are four types of coaxial cables:

1. Thicknet cables are 10-mm-thick coaxial cable. Used for the IEEE standard Ethernet 10Base5 networks, Thicknet cable has a speed of 10 Mb/s over a segment length range of 500 meters (Figure 3-5).
2. Thinnet cables are 5-mm coaxial cables that serve as an inexpensive alternative for Thicknet cables. Thinnet is used for the IEEE standard Ethernet 10Base2 network, and has a speed of 10 Mb/s over a segment length range of 200 meters (Figure 3-6).
3. *CATV*, an acronym for Community Antenna Television, is coaxial cabling used for transmission of cable TV signals; it is also used with Ethernet 10Broad36 networks.
4. *Twinax*, also called twin axial, is also one of the types of coaxial cables. It is communication cable, consisting of two solid center conductors surrounded by an insulating cover and shielded by a tubular outer conductor (can be a braid, foil, or both). The arrangement is then surrounded with an insulating and protective outer layer.

Fiber-Optic Cable

A fiber-optic cable is a flexible, thin glass fiber, which is surrounded by a plastic cover. Electrical signal is converted into optical signal and transmitted to the destination; it is reconverted into an electrical signal at the destination.

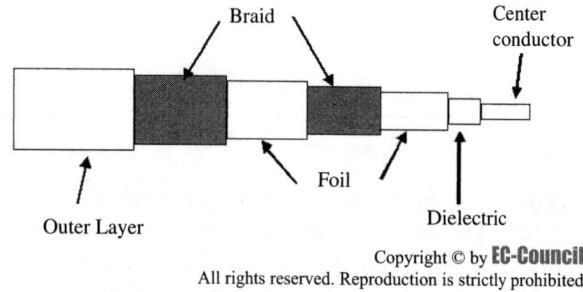

Figure 3-5 An interior view of Thicknet cable.

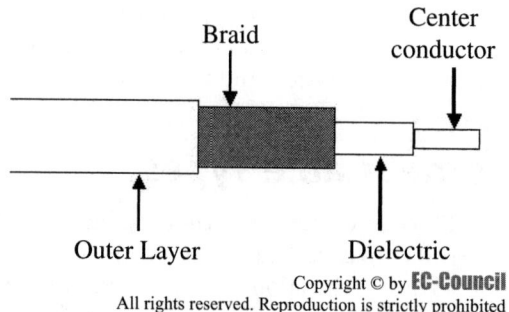

Figure 3-6 An interior view of Thinnet cable.

Optical cables are utilized in pairs, with one fiber of the pair transmitting the signal to the destination, and the other fiber carrying the signal in the other direction. This bidirectional communication is made possible by transmitting data at different wavelengths, and by employing appropriate coupling/splitting devices.

There are two types of optical fibers. *Multimode fiber (MMF)* allows multiple light signals to propagate through the fiber optic; a large core permits coupling from cheaper LEDs, couplers, and connectors. *Single-mode fiber (SMF)* transmits data from a single small light source.

The advantages of optical fiber include less data loss and large data-carrying capacity. Also, transmission is not interferred with by electromagnetic interference and nuclear electromagnetic pulses, electrical resistance is high, and cables weigh less.

Some disadvantages of fiber-optic cable include expensive cables, transmitters, and receivers that are susceptible to "fiber fuse" at higher optical powers, and peripherals that cannot rely on these cables for power; they cannot carry power.

Other Types of Ethernet LAN

Other types of Ethernet have been developed to enhance the performance and the speed of Ethernet LANs. *Switched Ethernet* is an enhanced version of the 10Base5 standard Ethernet model, where the hub in the star topology is replaced by a switch, which recognizes the destination address and transmits data to its respective destination, rather than broadcasting packets of data to all the computers in the network.

Fast Ethernet is a networking standard that supports data transfer rates up to 100 Mbps by decreasing the collision domain, the maximum distance data travels between two stations on a network. Because this standard is 10 times faster than 10BaseT Ethernet, it is often referred to as Fast Ethernet. Officially, the IEEE 802.3 standard is 100BaseT for data transfer rates up to 100 Mbps.

Gigabit Ethernet operates at 1000 Mb/s by reducing the collision domain. Gigabit Ethernet can be utilized properly if it is connected as the backbone to a Fast Ethernet network.

Virtual Private Network

A *virtual private network (VPN)* is a private network that is used in an organization, or by a group of organizations, to include, summarize, encrypt, and validate links across shared or public networks. A VPN uses an existing network to establish connections between terminals, and employs various cryptographic algorithms, tunneling techniques, and protocols to maintain privacy over the network. A secure VPN must include confidentiality to prevent snooping, sender authentication to prevent identity spoofing, and message integrity to prevent message alteration (Figure 3-7).

There are numerous benefits when using a VPN. It can extend geographic connectivity, improve security when data lines are not encrypted, and reduce operational costs when compared to a WAN. VPNs can also reduce transmission time and transportation costs for remote users, improve productivity, simplify network topology, and provide broadband networking compatibility. Finally, VPNs can provide a faster return on investment than a leased/owned WAN, reduce expansion costs, and are easily scalable when compared to other networks.

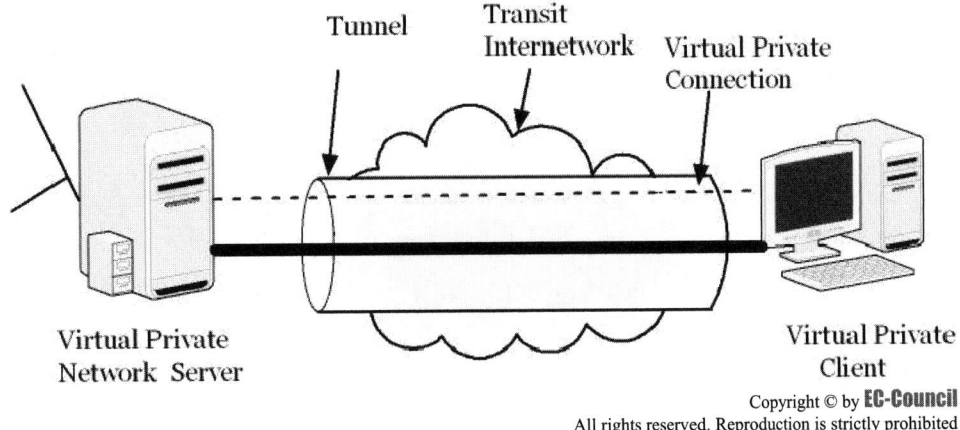

Figure 3-7 A VPN configuration.

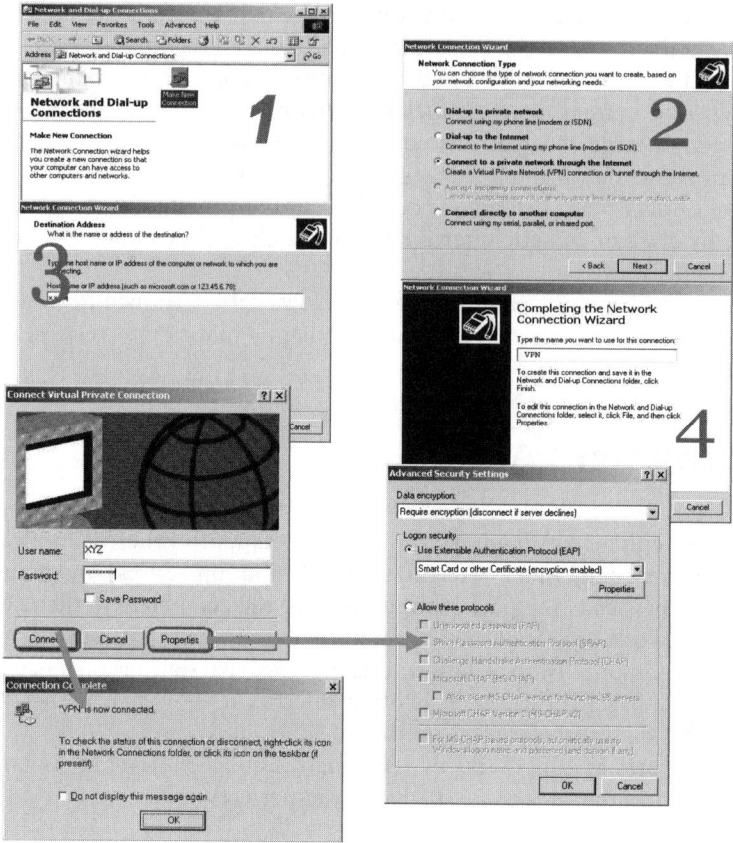

Figure 3-8 How to connect to a VPN.

Connecting to a VPN Using Windows 2000

To connect to a VPN (Figure 3-8):

1. Open **Network and Dial-up Connections.**
2. Double-click **Make New Connection,** and then click **Next.**
3. Click **Connect to a Private Network through the Internet,** and click **Next.**

If the connection is already established, then choose one of the following options:

1. If a new connection is to be established with an ISP, click the button beside **Automatically Dial this Initial Connection,** choose a connection from the list, and then click **Next;** otherwise
2. Click **Do not Dial the Initial Connection,** and then click **Next.**
3. Type the hostname or IP address of the computer or network in the text bar, to which a connection is to be established, and then click **Next.**

If this connection is to be made available to all users on a local network:

1. Click **For All Users,** and then click **Next.** Otherwise, click **Only for Myself,** and then click Next.
2. Select the check box beside **Enable Internet Connection Sharing for this Connection,** and then click **Next.**
3. Name the connection, and then click **Finish.**

Chapter Summary

- Ethernet is a LAN standard, technically known as IEEE 802.3.
- Ethernet is categorized into baseband and broadband.
- Baseband is divided into 10Base5, 10Base2, and 10Base-T standards; broadband's standard is 10Broad36.
- Different Ethernet cables include twisted-pair cable, coaxial cable, and fiber-optic cable.
- VPN is a private network used by organizations to communicate over a public network.

Review Questions

1. What is an Ethernet?

2. What is the minimum range/distance of an Ethernet? The maximum range/distance?

3. What kind of signal does baseband Ethernet use? How about broadband Ethernet?

4. What are the standards the IEEE 802.3 model specifies for baseband Ethernet?

5. How many IEEE 802.3 standards are specified for broadband Ethernet?

6. What are the category types of Ethernet cable?

7. Name three types of Ethernet LANs that have enhanced performance and speed.

8. What is a virtual private network?

9. Discuss the benefits of using VPNs.

10. What characteristics must a secure VPN include?

Hands-On Projects

1. Identify the type of Ethernet LAN in your classroom. What are its characteristics?
2. Identify 10Base5 Ethernet cable from a set of cables. What are the differences between the cables?
3. Try connecting computers on a network using 10Base2 Ethernet cable.

Chapter 4

Installation of Basic Hardware Components

Objectives

After completing this chapter, you should be able to:
- Understand basic hardware components
- Install a CPU
- Install a motherboard
- Configure a motherboard
- Install a power supply and a hard drive
- Know the definition and use of legacy devices
- Understand the process of configuring IDE/ATA and SCSI devices
- Understand ports
- Understand the process of detecting hardware devices

Key Terms

Advanced technology attachment (ATA)   the standard cable interface that is used for data storage devices

Arithmetic and logic unit (ALU)   performs arithmetic and logical operations in the CPU of a computer

ATX   outward appearance factor, or design and arrangement, of components on a motherboard

Basic input/output system (BIOS)   contains programming code allowing communication between the operating system and the computer's hardware

CD drive   compact disk drive used to store and retrieve data

Central processing unit (CPU)   the most important element of a computer; performs arithmetic/logic and extracts instructions from memory and executes them

Complementary metal oxide conductor (CMOS)   enables devices to consume extremely low levels of power

Control unit   unit that extracts instructions from memory and executes them using a program

Data cable a group of cables with a protective plastic covering
Device Manager a feature in Windows to monitor the installed hardware in a system
Direct memory access (DMA) assignments are connected to input devices and helps in faster accessing of data
Floppy drive a removable magnetic disk used for data storage
Hard drive a device used to permanently save, store, and retrieve information
Input/output (I/O) addresses represent memory location of devices to the CPU for information transfer
Integrated drive electronics (IDE) the cable interface used for hard disks and CD-ROMs
Jumper a metal link that is used to close an electrical circuit
Legacy devices non-plug-and-play devices
Motherboard the main circuit board of a computer; generally consists of the CPU, BIOS, memory, storage, interfaces, serial and parallel ports, expansion slots, and every controller required for standard peripheral devices like the monitor, keyboard, and hard disk
Port an interface for connecting devices to a computer
Power supply supplies power to a computer
Random access memory (RAM) a type of computer memory that can be accessed randomly
SCSI an interface used to connect peripherals to the computer
Zip drive a small, portable disk drive

Case Study

Shawn Roberts, a high school student, has a home PC, which he uses for playing games and browsing the Internet. One day, Shawn's friend, Randy, came over to his house and wanted to play the game AlphaZero on a floppy diskette. Shawn's system does not have a floppy drive, so he plans on buying one. With his favorite game in hand, Shawn is kicking himself over installing a floppy drive.

How would Shawn install his newly purchased floppy drive?

Introduction to Installation of Basic Hardware Components

This chapter will introduce and define the basic hardware components of a computer and how to install them. The complex configuration of legacy devices are detailed and broken down, types of ports are defined, and the benefits of Windows Device Manager are explored.

Basic Hardware Components

The average personal computer consists of basic hardware components. The ***motherboard***, sometimes referred to as the *mobo*, is the main circuit board of a computer. The motherboard generally consists of the ***central processing unit***, or ***CPU***, the most important element of a computer, which performs arithmetic/logic and and extracts instructions from memory and executes them; and ***BIOS***, the ***basic input/output system***, which contains programming code allowing communication between the operating system and the computer's hardware. The motherboard also contains memory, storage, interfaces, serial and parallel ports, expansion slots, and every controller required in controlling standard peripheral devices such as the monitor, keyboard, and the hard disk. All these chips reside on the surface of the motherboard; they are called the motherboard's chipset. In most computers, it is feasible to add memory chips directly to the motherboard. The user can also upgrade to a faster PC by changing the CPU chip. In order to add further core features, the user may need to replace the entire motherboard.

The ***power supply***, also called the power supply unit, or PSU, is the component that supplies power to a computer. For most computers, power supplies can be plugged into standard electrical outlets. The power supply then extracts the required amount of electricity and regulates the voltage to eliminate spikes and surges. PSUs are rated in terms of the number of watts they generate.

The CPU is often called the brains of a computer. The CPU is housed in a single chip called a microprocessor. There are two general components of a CPU. They are the ***arithmetic and logic unit***, which performs arithmetic and logical operations, and the ***control unit***, which extracts instructions from memory and executes them using a program.

Another basic hardware component is memory or **RAM,** *random access memory,* which is a type of computer memory that can be accessed randomly. It is the most customary type of memory found in computers. There are two types of RAM, known as dynamic RAM (DRAM) and static RAM (SRAM).

Finally, data storage devices can be fixed media such as a **hard drive,** a device used to permanently save, store, and retrieve information. Data can also be stored in removable media. **Floppy drives** are removable magnetic disks used for data storage. **CD drives** are compact disk drives that are used to store and retrieve data. **Zip drives** are small, portable disk drives.

Installing a CPU

Follow these steps to install a CPU:

1. Locate the processor socket on the motherboard and open the slot by pulling the lever on the side of the slot.
2. Find the keyed end of the processor that has the diagonal corner in the pin layout.
3. Arrange the processor to match the corner between the processor and the socket.
4. Ensure that all pins are lined up, and insert the socket so that all pins fit in the proper holes.
5. Lock the processor by lowering down the lifted slot.
6. Apply a thermal pad over the uncovered portion of the processor. If thermal paste is to be used, apply a thin layer of it.
7. Place the heat sink, or cooling solution, above the processor by aligning the clamps with the mounting points around the processor. Be careful while aligning the clamps; a single slip of the screwdriver can damage the motherboard.
8. Find the power lead for the cooling solution's fan and the CPU fan header on the motherboard. Plug the cooling solution fan power connector into the fan header on the board.

Installing a Motherboard

Before installing the motherboard, carefully read the instructions and information about the motherboard in its user manual. Modern **ATX,** the outward appearance factor, or design and arrangement, of components on a motherboard, come with a variety of connectors or **jumpers,** metal links that are used to close electrical circuits. To facilitate optimal operation of a computer, it is necessary to follow the layout given in the manual.

Follow these steps to install a motherboard:

1. Open the computer case.
2. Remove the motherboard tray.
3. Change the ATX connector plate.
4. Set the motherboard mounting location. There are a series of mounting holes between the case and the motherboard. Match the holes of the motherboard with the case and then mount it.
5. Place the screws to mount the motherboard.
6. Fix the motherboard.
7. Attach the ATX cabinet control wires/cables.
8. Connect it to the power supply.

Configuring a Motherboard

Before configuring a motherboard, it is necessary to understand how to manipulate jumpers. Typically, a jumper consists of a plastic plug that fits over a pair of protruding pins. Jumpers are sometimes used to configure expansion boards. By placing a jumper plug over a different set of pins, you can change a motherboard's parameters.

The jumpers are normally numbered as JP1, JP2, and so on. Each motherboard has a different jumper number, position, and most importantly, how the jumper settings are defined. To understand jumpers, the motherboard manual is very crucial. Today, jumperless motherboards are on the market. With these types of jumperless motherboards, settings such as CPU type and speed, CPU voltage, and BIOS settings can be done without even opening the case.

A few things should be kept in mind: When setting the processor speed via the jumpers, use the processor's *true* speed. Chips that have the P-rating system do not run at true speed. The P-rating is nothing but a comparison to the Intel chip. An example is the AMD K5-166. This chip has a P-rating of 166 MHz, but actually runs at 116.7 MHz.

Several precautions are recommended when configuring a motherboard:

- When setting the jumpers, place the board on the static bag it came in.
- Always keep the board on a flat surface.
- Always ground yourself before handling the board.
- Handle the board by the edges only.

Follow these steps to configure a motherboard:

1. Follow the user manual provided. Always look at the listings for settings; identify all jumpers on the motherboard itself and what settings they control.
2. Set the voltage settings. Most older chips use one single voltage; the newer chips used today employ a split voltage. Modern motherboards provide jumpers for the core voltage and I/O voltage. Set the voltages according to the CPU.
3. Set the processor speed. A single jumper cannot perform this task since it requires setting the system bus speed and a multiplier. The multiplier is the number, when multiplied by the system bus speed, which gives the processor speed. For each of these settings, there is a separate jumper. Configure these jumpers according to the CPU.
4. Set the **CMOS**, a *complementary metal oxide semiconductor* that enables devices to consume extremely low levels of power; clear jumper to normal so the BIOS settings can be changed later.
5. Set the battery jumper to onboard battery instead of external battery.
6. Disable the flash BIOS.
7. Check that all jumpers are set correctly.

Installing Power Supply

The power supply is the foremost factor in the proper functioning of a computer. In the case of most computers, power supplies can be plugged into standard electrical outlets. Extreme caution must be observed when installing the power supply in a computer.

Follow these steps to install the power supply:

1. Open the computer cabinet.
2. Align the power supply unit with the holes.
3. Fix the power supply into the cage.
4. Set the voltage switch to a proper voltage level.
5. Fix the power supply to the motherboard.
6. Attach the cable from the PSU (power supply unit) to all devices.

Installing a Hard Drive

Hard drives are classified as either primary or secondary. The installation process is almost the same; the only difference lies in the jumper settings. In primary, the jumper mode setting is referred to as *master*; in secondary, it is known as *slave*. Before installing a hard drive, it is essential to determine the configuration required.

If there is already an existing hard drive and it is configured as master, then set the new hard drive to slave mode. If an existing drive is set for *cable select*, then set the new drive to cable-select mode as well. Always change the jumper setting to suit the required configuration.

Follow these steps to install a primary hard drive:

1. Shut down the system.
2. Unplug the power cord.
3. Open the computer case.

4. In most PCs, if there is a single drive, select the cable-select option. If there is another drive, select the master setting.

5. Insert the drive into the case, match the holes, and fasten the screws.

6. Plug the *IDE* cable, also known as an *integrated drive electronics* cable interface that is used for hard disks and CD-ROMs, to the motherboard. These IDE cables are usually ATA/66 and ATA/100, or *advanced technology attachment*, the standard cable interface that is used for data storage devices. They have a blue connector, or a connector labeled System Board, which is plugged into either the IDE0 (primary) or IDE1 (secondary) connector on the motherboard.

7. Key the cables, if possible. If the cable is not keyed, make sure that the red stripe on the IDE cable matches up to pin 1 on the motherboard.

8. Fix the farthest connector, either black in color or labeled primary, to the hard drive. Fix the middle connector to the secondary drive, if present. Make sure that the cable with the red stripe is the connector on the hard drive.

9. Find a free 4-pin Molex connector from the power supply and plug into the power connector on the hard drive.

10. Close the case and plug in the power cord.

Installing Floppy and CD/DVD Drives

During the installation of a floppy drive, the method of sliding can differ depending on the cage. The two methods for installation are sliding rails or directly inserting into the cage.

Follow these steps to install a floppy drive:

1. Shut down the computer and unplug the cord.
2. Open the computer case.
3. Install the floppy cable with a twist at the end to make it drive A.
4. Find the floppy connector, which is smaller in size than the IDE connector.
5. Locate the edge of the ribbon with red wire and place this on the side of the motherboard connector with the pin 1 indicator.
6. Plug one end of the floppy drive cable into the board.
7. Attach the other end to the floppy drive.
8. Connect it to the power supply cable.
9. Connect the floppy drive using its cable to the motherboard.

Follow these steps to install a CD/DVD drive:

1. Unplug the power cord.
2. Remove the computer case.
3. Place the CD/DVD/CDRW-ROM drive in a free half-height drive with a 5.25" slot.
4. Slide the drive into the disc tray opening that's facing the front of the computer.
5. Close the computer case.

It is advisable to install a CD/DVD drive only on the secondary IDE BUS using its own IDE cable; keep the jumper in master mode. In the primary IDE BUS, set the hard drive in master mode, and set the CD/DVD drive in slave mode. In slave mode, the CD/DVD drive shares the IDE cable with the hard drive, which can degrade the performance of the system.

Legacy Devices

Legacy devices are non-plug-and-play. Understanding the configuration of legacy devices is complex, but can be made easier by understanding the concepts and terms related to them.

There are three basic types of hardware resources:

1. Interrupt request (IRQ) line assignments allow devices a direct line to the CPU (Figure 4-1).

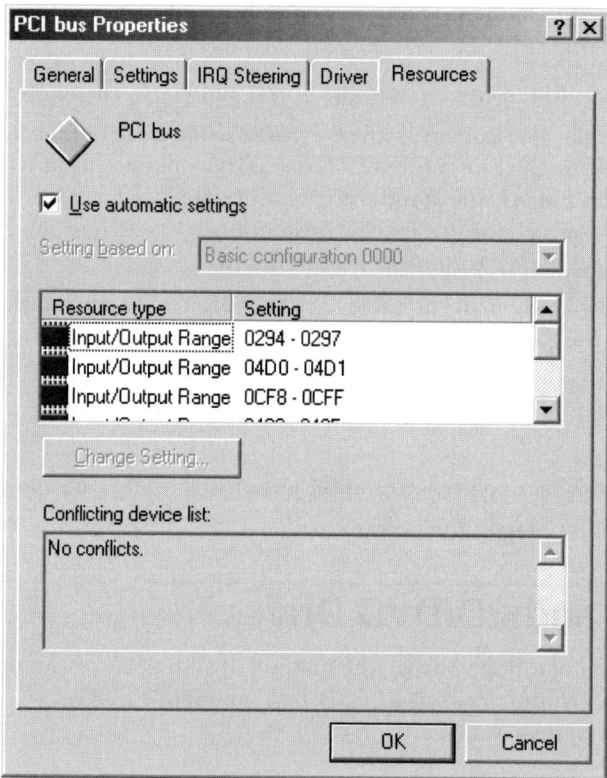

Figure 4-1 The CPU responds to IRQ signals in numerical order.

2. *Direct memory access (DMA)* assignments are connected to input devices and help in faster accessing of data.

3. *Input/output (I/O) addresses* represent memory locations of devices to the CPU for information transfer.

Why is it necessary to understand these devices?

Sometimes situations arise when two or more devices are utilizing the same resource, which gives rise to device conflict. Conflicting situations can gain normal positioning if one or more devices stop utilizing the resource. But, this situation can become worse if the devices do not stop utilizing the resource. Understanding hard devices plays a vital role in managing such problems.

Interrupt Request Line Assignments

Dedicated signal lines or circuits between the system CPU and hardware devices are known as interrupt request lines (IRQ) or hardware interrupts. These signal lines serve the purpose of informing the CPU that the allocated device needs processor attention. The CPU gets the alert and responds to the situation by stopping its current operation and shifting its attention to the "interrupting" device. These are also known as *maskable interrupts*; the computer can ignore the interrupts until it finishes its current task.

Direct Memory Access

Direct Memory Access (DMA) is a function to access RAM directly for peripherals and integrated hardware components. The CPU is not interrupted for access, which increases the system's speed. DMA is commonly used for floppy disk drives, sound cards, and tape drives. But, if device conflict occurs, it is very difficult to examine it on DMA.

Before enabling DMA for a hard disk, it is essential to determine whether DMA is enabled on the computer. Use *Device Manager*, a feature in Windows to monitor the installed hardware in a system, to check the resource status. To enable DMA for a hard disk, the latest driver for the motherboard that provides DMA support must be installed.

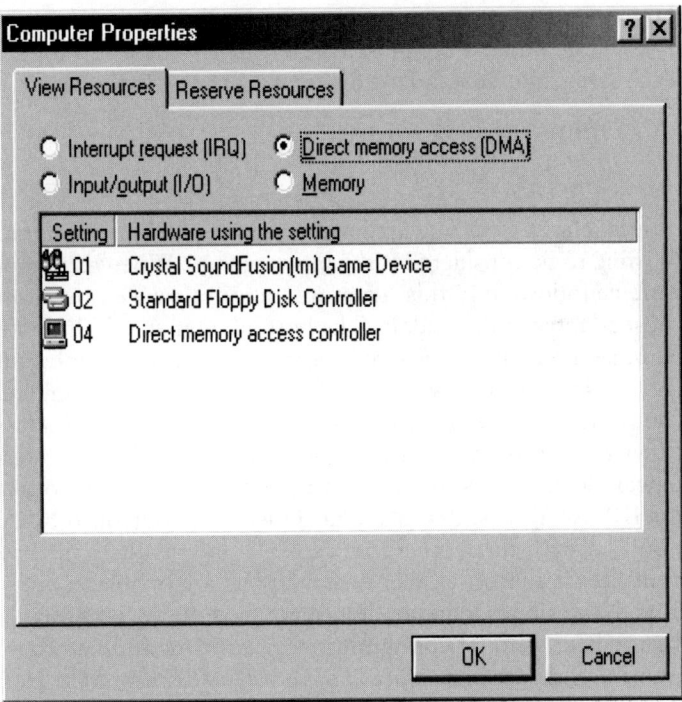

Figure 4-2 DMA must be enabled for CD-ROM use.

Follow these steps to enable DMA for CD-ROM (Figure 4-2):

1. Go to **Start** → **Settings** → **Control Panel** → **Systems**.
2. Go to the **Device Manager** tab and double click **CD-ROM** after expanding it.
3. Go to the **Settings** tab, check the **DMA** check box, and click **OK**.
4. Restart the computer.

Input/Output Addresses

Each device present in a computer uses an input/output (I/O) address, which represents the memory location of a device to the CPU for information transfer. These addresses are expressed in hexadecimal notation. Each device is called and identified by its address, by the CPU. The CPU communicates with its printer using address 378h.

I/O addresses vary in size, when compared to the uniform size of IRQs and DMA channels, because some devices, like network cards, have much more information to move around than other devices, like keyboards. The size of the I/O address is determined by the design of the card, and for compatibility with older devices.

Most devices utilize an I/O address space of 4, 8, or 16 bytes; some use as few as 1 byte, and others as many as 32 or more. The wide discrepancy in the size of the I/O addresses can make it difficult to determine and resolve resource conflicts; I/O addresses are often referred to only by the first byte of the I/O address.

Configuring IDE/ATA Devices

The configuration of separate IDE/ATA devices in a system is important because setup can have a strong impact on a PC's optimal performance. Configuration should always begin with the drive's manual for each step.

Follow these steps to configure IDE/ATA devices:

1. Determining the right configuration is necessary. A system with one hard disk and one CD-ROM is generally configured with the hard disk as the master drive on the primary channel, and the CD-ROM as the master drive on the secondary channel.
2. Determine which drives need jumpering. Double-check the configuration of the new drives being added to the system to match it with the system configuration plan. Existing drives do not require rejumpering.

3. Determine how to jumper each device. There are various points to consider; many drives jumper only as master or slave, while others have master, slave, and "single" configurations. It is better to make a CD-ROM master. There is no set standard for jumpering IDE/ATA hard disk drives.
4. Set jumpers for each device.

SCSI Devices

There are various issues related to setting up devices utilizing *SCSI*, an interface used to connect peripherals to a computer. The first thing to be considered is the bus topology. When setting up a SCSI topology, it is important that a chain structure be followed. In this structure, internal devices are at one end, external devices are at the other end, with a host adapter in the middle. The host adapter should have its termination disabled.

Device IDs must be set up to avoid resource conflicts. A specific number should be used for addressing each SCSI device on the bus. Narrow SCSI with up to 8 devices should be numbered 0 to 7; wide SCSI with up to 16 devices should be numbered 0 to 15. SCSI awards priority by ID number. For narrow SCSI, 7 is the highest and 0 is the lowest. For wide SCSI, the priority sequence is 7, 6, 5, 4, 3, 2, 1, 0, 15, 14, 13, 12, 11, 10, 9, and 8.

SCSI utilizes logical block addressing to identify devices, and does not rely on the system BIOS for geometry information, as IDE/ATA does. But, SCSI hard disks are controlled by the internal SCSI BIOS on the host adapter, so issues built-in with the motherboard's BIOS will result. Limitations of the host adapter BIOS can affect access to the devices it controls. Older host adapters are unable to access hard disks over 1 GB in size, or other arbitrary limits. Newer host adapters should not have these limitations.

To eliminate the need for manual configuration of jumpers and switches, protocol has been developed to automate the assignment of device IDs, called *Plug and Play SCSI* or *SCAM*. But, this protocol does not always work reliably. Problems can arise if devices supporting SCAM are mixed with other devices that do not support the feature.

Safe BIOS Settings

Using safe settings for the basic input/output system (BIOS) ensures proper functioning between the operating system and the computer's hardware. To begin, locate the entry in the BIOS setup menu for autodetecting the hard disk (Figure 4-3). Set up the system's basic parameters by checking standard settings such as date and time. Use the mm/dd/yy format for date and the 24-hour clock for time.

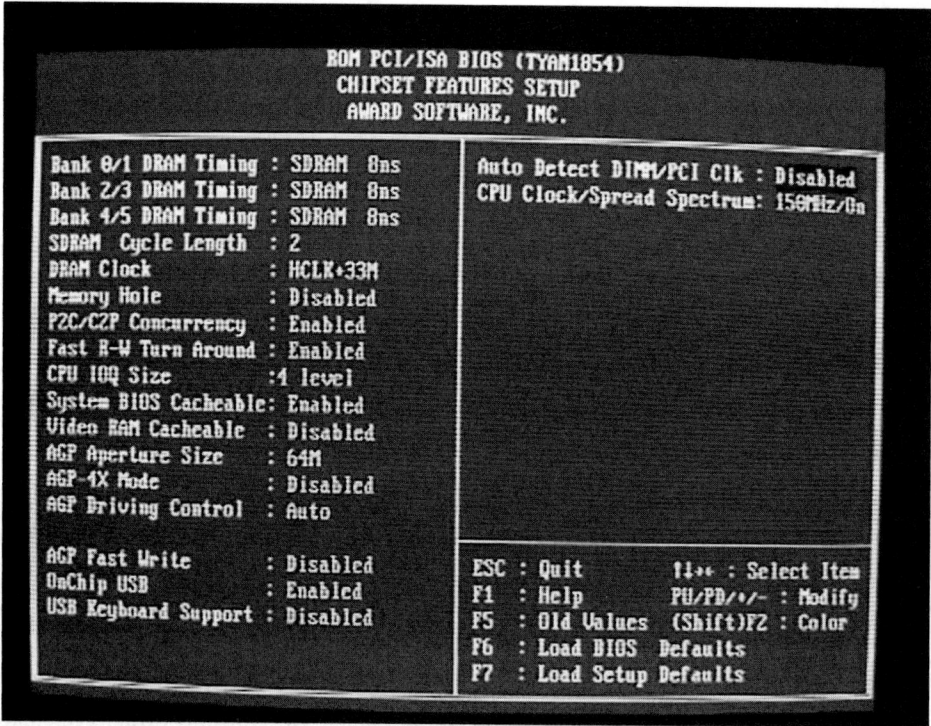

Figure 4-3 BIOS setup screen.

Follow these steps after accessing BIOS setup procedure:

1. Check settings of primary and secondary, slave and master.
2. Set User for hard disk and set CD-ROM for CD drive. Set the correct type for the floppy drive(s) in the system.
3. Set translation mode to LBA for newer hard disks, and Normal or CHS for older hard disks.
4. Disable the block mode.
5. Set VGA/EGA for video display.
6. Set auto virus detection and enable external caches.

After setting, go to main menu, choose the save option, and exit the BIOS setup procedure. This requires rebooting the system. For newer systems, be sure that the floppy boot disk is still in the floppy drive so the system will boot from it.

CMOS

CMOS technology, or complementary metal oxide semiconductor, uses power when the transistor switches between on-off states. This technology deals with chip power consumption and heat dissipation. CMOS is the place where basic data for a computer is set up to start the system correctly. The CMOS setup procedure can be accessed by entering the BIOS screen; choose the first option, which is Standard CMOS Setup. Date and time may be already set; if not, set this by using the arrow keys to move, and PageUp/PageDown to modify the highlighted item.

Set the BIOS to automatically detect the hard disks each time the computer is booted up. Set hard disks to User. This option will scan for the current disk in that position and set the columns automatically.

Set the following for CMOS:

1. Primary Master, mode Auto
2. Primary Slave, mode Auto
3. Secondary Slave, Auto
4. Secondary Slave, Auto

Understanding Ports

A *port* can be defined as an interface for connecting devices to a computer. Ports can be located at the back of a computer. They permit the computer to access external devices, such as a printer. A commonly used port, in terms of the Internet, is port 80, which is the http port.

There are four common types of ports. A serial port, also known as a COM port, is an interface used to connect a serial device to a computer. RS-232c and RS-422 are the serial ports for connecting a mouse and modem. LPT, or line printer terminal, is a 25-pin parallel port, used for connecting printers.

A USB, or universal serial bus, port is used for USB devices. USB is a computer standard, capable of transferring data at the rate of 12 Mbps, and can support up to 127 peripheral devices. Firewire ports, also known as IEEE 1394 or iLink, support up to 63 devices, with a maximum bandwidth of 400 Mbps.

Data Cables

Data cables are a group of cables with a protective plastic covering. There are a variety of data cables available to suit specific devices and ports.

Ribbon cables are generally used for devices such as CD-ROM or hard disk drives. They are thin cables with dotted or striped lines that look similar to a car's seat belt. The dotted or striped lines help in identifying the pinned edge, and assist the user in connecting the cable properly. Today, most ribbon cables are also keyed, allowing the cable to only be connected one way. The ribbon cable for floppy drives has a 34-pin socket, and a split and twist in the ribbon close to the connector.

SCSI cables are used for connecting a SCSI device to a SCSI controller. This cable is generally a wide, flat cable, or it may also look rounded. SCSI cables often have multiple connections on a single cable, which permit multiple devices to hook up to a single controller.

The null modem cable is used to directly connect two computers without using a modem. This cable connects to the computer serial port, and has the ability to communicate by crossing the sending and receiving cables within one cable. It is also known as an RS-232 cable.

Connectors

A connector is the part of a cable that plugs into a port, or interface, to connect one device to another. Most connectors are either *male* (containing one or more exposed pins) or *female* (containing holes in which the male connector can be inserted).

DB connectors are serial and parallel depending on the type of cable that is used. Commonly used connectors are the DB-9, DB-15, DB-19, DB-25, DB-37, and DB-50. The number stands for the number of active lines in the connector. The DB-9 and DB-15 are found on serial ports and network cards. Sometimes, the DB-9 cable is used for Token-Ring adapters; the DB-15 is used for Thicknet coaxial cables.

DIN connectors match a standard defined by the DIN Group, and are used for computer keyboards, computer mice, network routers, video appliances, and Apple serial devices. The PS2 connector is specifically used for mice. USB connectors are used for USB devices.

RJ11 and RJ45 are other important connectors used in small networks, or LANs. An RJ-11 is a four- or six-wire connection, which is mainly used for telephones and computer modem connectors; RJ-45 has 8 pins and is used on Ethernet twisted-pair links.

Detecting Hardware Devices

Hardware can cause problems in a computer's performance, so it is sometimes necessary to detect the hardware on a system and track its function status. In Windows, Device Manager can be used for this purpose. It is a feature to monitor the installed hardware in a system.

The configuration of hardware can also be changed using Device Manager. Normally, Device Manager is used to check the status of computer hardware and update device drivers on a computer. However, a thorough understanding of computer hardware concepts allows the user to exploit the Device Manager's diagnostic features to solve device clashes and change resource settings.

Device Manager can be used to:

- Identify the hardware present in the system.
- Change hardware configuration.
- Install updated drivers.
- Identify device conflicts.
- Change properties and settings of devices.
- Disable, enable, and uninstall devices.
- Reinstall the previous version of a driver.
- Enable the user to print a summary of the devices that are installed on a computer.

Using Device Manager

Device Manager can be accessed by using any of the following methods.

1. The user can run the program by entering its filename in the following way (Figure 4-4):

    Start -> Run -> Type devmgmt.msc

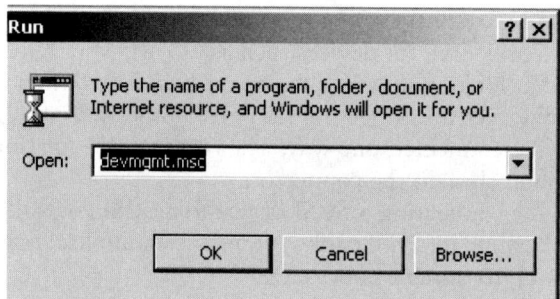

Figure 4-4 The user can run Device Manager by entering its filename.

2. The user can also open Device Manager through the following method (Figure 4-5):

   Right-click **My Computer** -> **Manage** -> **Device Manager**

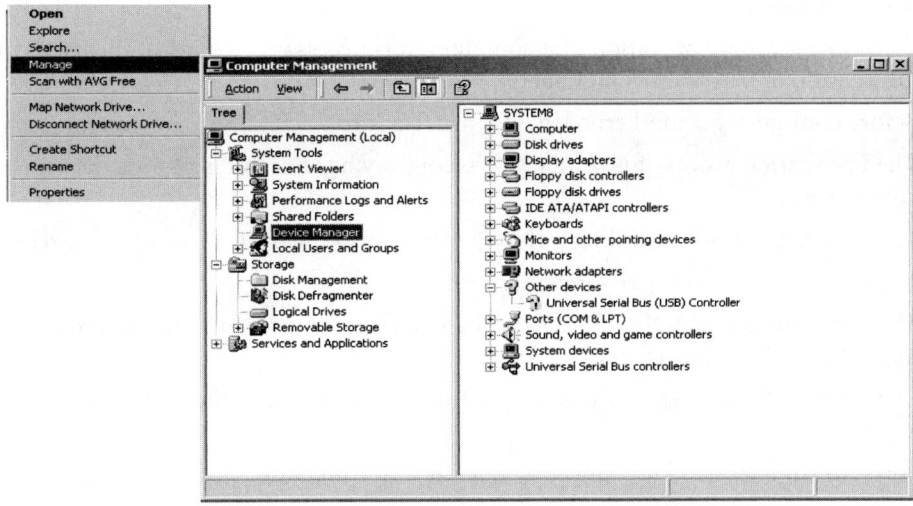

Figure 4-5 The user can also open Device Manager through this method.

3. Finally, Device Manager can be accessed by this method as well (Figure 4-6):

   Right-click **My Computer** -> **Properties** -> **Hardware** tab -> **Device Manager**

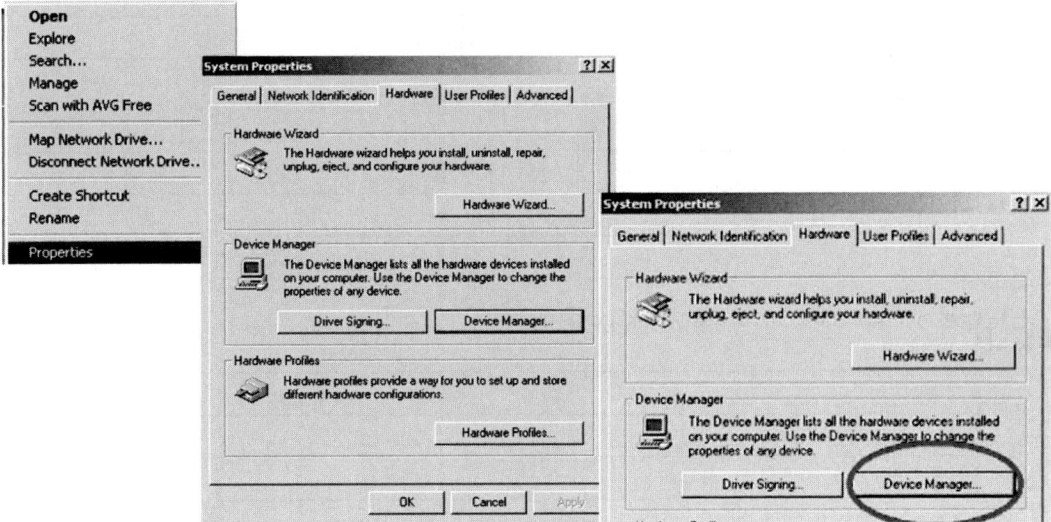

Figure 4-6 Device Manager can be accessed by this method as well.

Chapter Summary

- Basic hardware components include the motherboard, the power supply, the CPU, memory, and storage devices.
- To facilitate proper operation of a computer, it is necessary to consult the user's manual before any installation of hardware components.
- Before configuring a motherboard, it is necessary to understand how to manipulate jumpers.
- The installation process for primary or secondary hard drives is almost the same; the difference is in the jumper settings.
- The two methods for installing a floppy drive are sliding rails or inserting directly into the cage.
- Legacy devices are non-plug-and-play devices.
- The configuration of IDE/ATA devices in a system is important because proper setup can have a strong impact on a PC's optimal performance.
- Using safe BIOS settings ensures proper functioning between the operating system and the hardware in a computer.
- Ports are an interface for connecting devices to a computer.
- In Windows, Device Manager can detect the hardware on a system, and its function status.

Review Questions

1. What is the motherboard's function in a computer system?

2. What is the most important element of a computer?

3. List two categories for data storage devices.

4. What are jumpers, and how are they used?

5. What must be determined before installing a hard drive?

6. Why is it necessary to understand legacy devices?

7. What are the issues to be concerned with when setting up SCSI devices?

8. Define the four most common types of ports.

9. Describe the physical characteristics of ribbon, SCSI, and null modem cables.

10. What is a connector?

11. What Windows feature can be used to monitor the installed hardware in a computer system?

Hands-On Projects

1. Set up the BIOS on your personal computer.
2. Check to see whether DMA is enabled on your system.
3. Identify the cable used for your printer and the port that it is plugged into.
4. Open the troubleshooting dialog box using Device Manager on your computer.

Chapter 5

Network Connectivity

Objectives

After completing this chapter, you should be able to:

- Set up a small network
- Know how to connect computers
- Utilize IP addressing
- Choose the most appropriate network service
- Determine how to decide on a network architecture
- Understand various Internet access technologies
- Make a dial-up connection
- Understand the types of file sharing
- Configure shared folder permissions

Key Terms

Default share a type of folder sharing that requires no configuration apart from the share designation

Domain Name Service (DNS) developed by the Internet Engineering Task Force (IETF) to standardize a way to map pairings of logical hostnames to actual IP addresses on a TCP/IP address

Dynamic Host Configuration Protocol (DHCP) based on a client/server model, it is programmed to run on a server, such as a system currently running Windows NT server; the DHCP client runs on a network client, such as a workstation currently running Windows 95 or Windows NT Workstation

File sharing sharing of data over a network

IP address computers/devices connected on a TCP/IP network are identified by this special 32-bit address

PCI a local bus that assists high-speed connection with peripherals

Restricted share a type of folder sharing that contains more restrictions than a default share

SOHO small office/home office

Windows Internet Name Service (WINS) an additional choice for determining hostnames on networks that utilize Microsoft TCP/IP; it offers a distributed database for recording and inquiring dynamic computer name-to-IP address mappings in a routed network environment. WINS utilizes the NetBIOS computer name for any Windows-based network client to record each client in the WINS database on a computer running on Windows NT server.

Case Study

Liza works at a firm that allows her to work from home part-time. She would like to use her home PC and connect her company laptop to the Internet at the same time. Her home PC is on a DSL, or digital subscriber line, and her partner uses another laptop that needs to be connected to the Internet as well.

How can Liza configure a small network to provide access to the Internet and have limited access between her home PC and her laptop?

Setting Up a Small Network

Increased everyday usage of computers is making us dependent on this high technology. Work that usually took days to complete is now finished in seconds. Because of their many advantages, small networks have now become a way of life for almost everyone utilizing technology in the home and office.

Before installing a *SOHO* (small office/home office) network, hardware requirements must be determined. A network card needs to be installed in the computer so it can be connected to a network. The most commonly used cards are PCI 10BaseT/100BaseT. Commonly used network cables include CAT5, UTP, and STP. Finally, signal distributors control data flow and have the ability to transfer data, connecting at speeds ranging from 10 MBits/s to 100 MBits/s.

Depending on the network, Liza has to decide whether to use a hub or a switch as signal distributor. Hubs forward data packets to all the computers connected in a network. Switches determine the MAC address of the recipient and send data packets to the designated computer on the network.

Connecting Computers

As technology advances, a computer user's hardware and software needs are constantly evolving. Hardware, such as the network card, and various software, or programs that run in the computer, require frequent updating.

Hardware Installation

Follow these steps to install hardware:

1. Turn off the computer.
2. Unplug the power cord.
3. Open the computer case.
4. Remove the bracket from a free *PCI*, a local bus that assists high-speed connection with peripherals, slot on the back of the system.
5. Insert the network card vertically into the slot. Push it in firmly, not forcefully.
6. Fasten the card by using the screw on the bracket.
7. Close the case.
8. Plug the power cord back in.

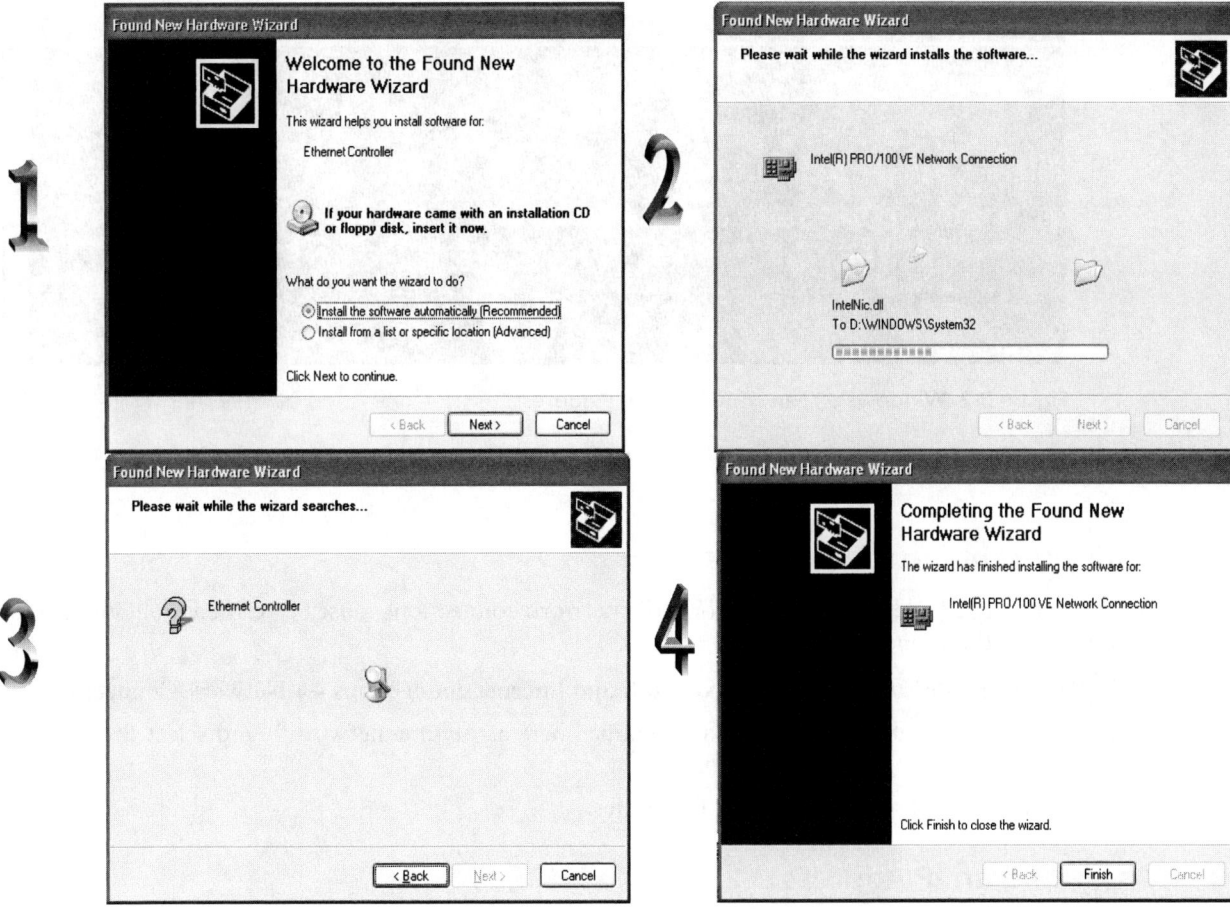

Figure 5-1 Windows displays the Found New Hardware Wizard to assist in installation.

Software Installation

Follow these steps to install software (Figure 5–1):

1. The Found New Hardware Wizard starts when new software is detected.
2. Select **Install the software automatically (Recommended)**.
3. Insert the disk received from the software manufacturer to choose the driver.
4. Windows searches for the driver.
5. Software is installed and ready to use when the driver installation is done.

IP Addressing

Computers and devices connected on a TCP/IP network are identified by a special 32-bit address called an *IP address*. IP addresses are categorized as both public and private to effectively route data packets in a network. This categorization process also ensures that the IP addresses of host machines in a network do not conflict with anyone's Internet address. The IP address of a computer running the Windows operating system can be found by typing in `ipconfig` at the command prompt (Figure 5-2).

```
C:\WINNT\system32\cmd.exe

C:\>ipconfig

Windows 2000 IP Configuration

Ethernet adapter Local Area Connection:

        Connection-specific DNS Suffix  . :
        IP Address. . . . . . . . . . . . : 192.168.0.6
        Subnet Mask . . . . . . . . . . . : 255.255.255.0
        Default Gateway . . . . . . . . . : 192.168.0.1

C:\>
```

Figure 5-2 Windows screen showing the IP address.

Verifying the Connection

Before assigning IP addresses in a network, the network connections must be verified. Follow this sequence of steps to verify the connection (Figure 5-3):

1. Press **Start → Control Panel → Network and Internet connections → Network Connections**.
2. Right-click **Local Area Connection** (renamed here as "Home network") and select **Properties** from the menu to view the Internet protocol.
3. Select **Internet Protocol** and click **Properties**.

Assigning an IP Address

All computer devices connected to the network need an IP address. They can be assigned manually or through an automated process called DHCP. Follow these steps to assign the IP addresses manually (Figure 5-4):

1. Select **Use the following IP address,** and then type the desired class of IP address.
2. Type in the default gateway and the DNS, or Domain Name System, servers, as given by the ISP.
3. Click **OK,** and then click **Close**.

To share a single Internet connection, Liza will need to install another NIC card on her home system. She can give the internal IP of the home computer to other computers on her network as the default gateway to share the Internet connection (Figure 5-4).

Adding Computers to a Workgroup

The next step in setting up a small network is assigning all LAN computers to a workgroup, which will allow easy sharing of network resources.

Follow these steps to add computers to a workgroup (Figure 5-5):

1. Right-click on **My Computer**.
2. Select **Properties**.
3. Select the **Computer Name** tab and enter the computer description.
4. Click **Change** to define the computer name and workgroup.
5. Enter the computer name and workgroup name in the fields provided.
6. Click **OK** and restart.

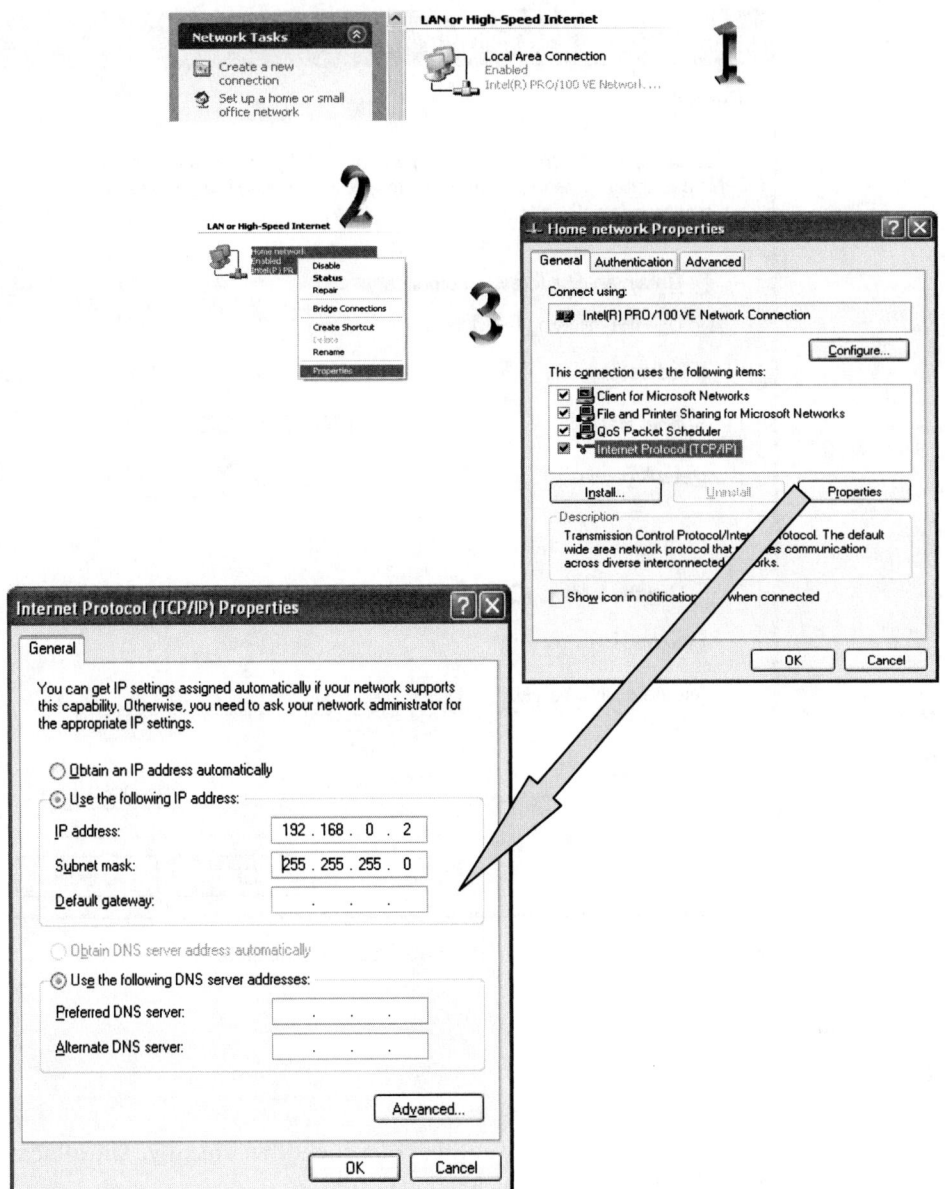

Figure 5-3 Steps to verify a network connection.

Network Services

A network administrator must choose the most appropriate network service to provide shared resources to client computers in a SOHO environment, or larger setting. The three most common network services will be discussed in this section; they all assist in managing IP addressing in various ways.

DHCP

Dynamic Host Configuration Protocol, or *DHCP,* is based on a client-server model. The DHCP server is programmed to run on a server, such as a system running a Windows Server operating system version. The DHCP client runs on a network client, such as a workstation currently running a Windows Server operating system version.

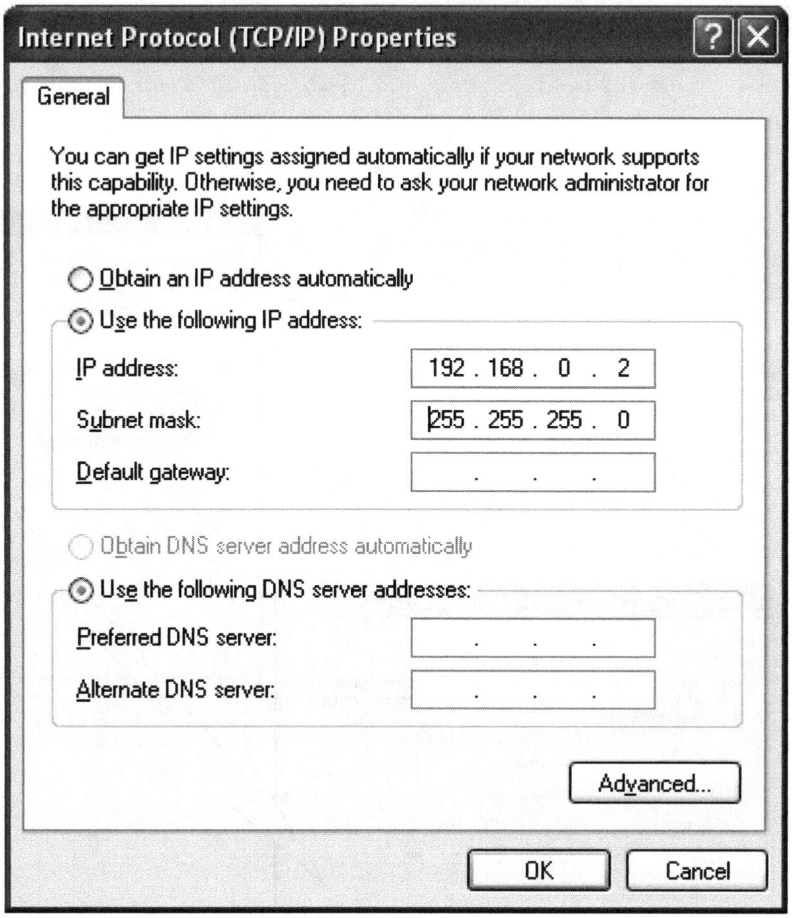

Figure 5-4 Steps to assign an IP address in a network.

DHCP is an IP standard that allocates the IP address of a client dynamically. The allocation is done from the IP database, located in the DHCP server, on the local network.

The advantages of a DHCP server are reliability and easier client configuration.

WINS

Windows Internet Name Service, or WINS, is an additional choice for determining hostnames on networks that utilize Microsoft TCP/IP. It offers a distributed database for recording and inquiring dynamic computer name-to-IP address mappings in a routed network environment. WINS utilizes the NetBIOS computer name for any Windows-based network client to record each client in the WINS database on a computer running on Windows NT server. WINS determines the IP address associated with a particular computer on a network, and provides support for network client and server computers that run on a Windows operating system. The distributed database automatically updates the names of computers currently available on a network, and the IP address assigned to each one.

DNS

Domain Name Service, or DNS, was developed by the Internet Engineering Task Force (IETF) was an attempt to standardize a way to map pairings of logical hostnames to actual IP addresses on a TCP/IP address. It is an Internet directory service. E-mail delivery is controlled by DNS; if a computer cannot access DNS, the Web browser will fail to find websites, and e-mail communication will fail as well.

The DNS system is made up of data including resource records, server, name server names and Internet Protocol adresses.

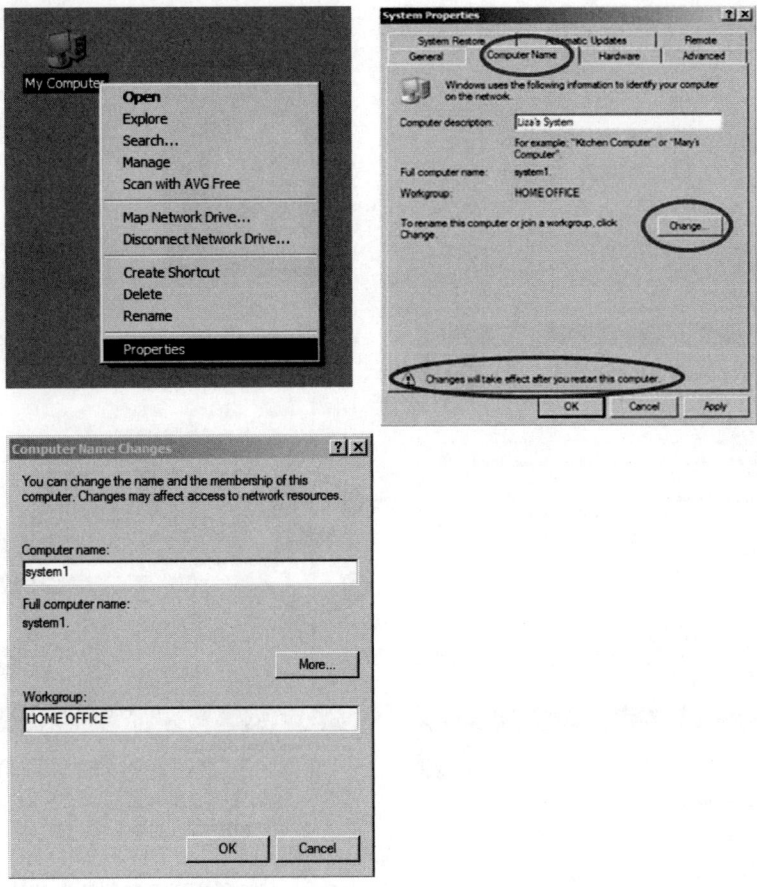

Figure 5-5 Steps to add a computer to a workgroup.

Deciding on a Network Architecture

Network architecture, or topology, refers to the configuration of cables, computers, and other peripherals. It is the geometric representation of the relationship of all the links and nodes to each other.

There are several issues to consider when choosing a topology:

- *Communication requirements*: Communication needs should be determined. What kind of data will need to be transmitted? Will high-end communication equipment be used, which requires greater bandwidth?
- *Financial feasibility*: Network architecture should make sense in terms of expenditure. For example, a linear bus network may be the least expensive way to install a network; this topology does not require purchasing concentrators.
- *Length of cable required*: A linear bus network employs shorter lengths of cable than other network topologies.
- *Scalability*: The network should be scalable so there would be no need of redeploying the architecture in case new systems are added. Expansion of a network is easier in a star topology, which easily accommodates adding another concentrator.
- *Cable type*: Unshielded twisted pair is the most common cable, often used with star topologies.

Internet Access Technology

Internet access is available through various ISP models. The ISP offers Internet connection by using specific data transmission technology appropriate for different Internet protocols, such as xDSL, broadband cable, wireless technology, and dial-up connections.

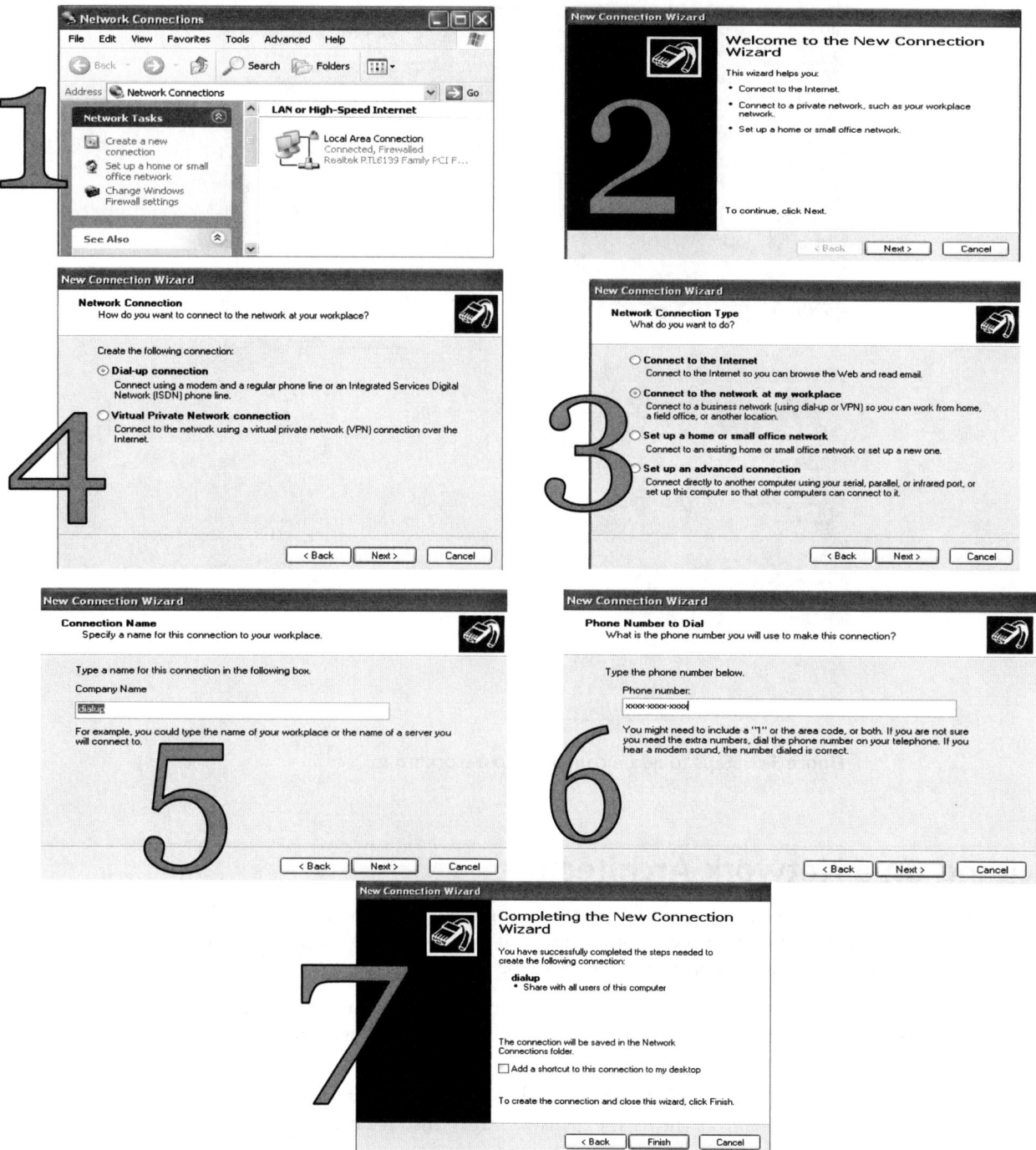

Figure 5-6 Steps to make a dial-up connection.

xDSL

A common term for the many combinations of DSL, or Digital Subscriber Line technology, xDSL has two main categories, known as ADSL and SDSL. xDSL is circuit-oriented, which makes each connection dependent on the other. The speed range for xDSL goes up to 32 Mbps for upstream traffic, and from 32 Kbps to over 1 Mbps for downstream traffic. For home users, speed ranges from 128 Kb/s to 1.5 Mb/s.

Type of equipment, distances involved, and cabling quality are a few factors that determine the speed of xDSL. This type of ISP provides greater bandwidth for sending and receiving information than other technologies available.

Broadband Cable

The cable TV network connection in a home runs through a cable modem, or broadband cable. It usually provides a bandwidth range up to 30 Mb/s from the service provider to the subscriber. Broadband cable is designed to be *broad;* each user receives the same signal. Cable TV networks follow a hierarchical topology in data transmission, requiring a downstream path and an upstream path.

Wireless

Wireless technology can provide access to a large number of subscribers in a wide geographic area. It works via a satellite TV service provider or a cellular phone network. Bandwidth for this technology can range from a few kilobits a second to many megabits. Wireless ISP architecture can be either symmetrical or asymmetrical.

Dial-Up Connection

This type of ISP connects a device to a network via a modem and a public telephone network. A dial-up connection utilizes normal telephone lines, but the quality of the connection is not always good. Dial-up access is similar to a phone connection, but the parties at the two ends are computer devices, not people. Previously, the maximum data rate with dial-up access was 56 Kbps (56,000 bits per second), but speed has improved with new technologies such as ISDN, or Integrated Services Digital Network.

Steps to Make a Dial-Up Connection

Liza wants to access the Internet using her dial-up connection. She sets up the connection successfully. Follow these steps to create a dial-up connection (Figure 5-6):

1. Click the **Start** button and go to Control Panel.
2. Open Network Connections and under **Network Tasks**, click **Create a new connection.**
3. The New Connection Wizard is activated.
4. Click **Next** and select **Connect to the network at my workplace.**
5. The Dial-up connection box appears when the **Next** button is clicked.
6. In the wizard, select **Dial-up connection.**
7. Enter the name for the dial-up connection.
8. Enter the phone number of the ISP and click **Next** to finish.

File Sharing

Sharing of data over a network is also called *file sharing*. Once files are shared on a network, they are called shared files. The owner of a file can limit access to other users. Access to shared files can be regulated by password protection, account or security authorizations, or locking the file to avoid simultaneous changes being made by more than one user at a time.

The term *file sharing* also refers to users being allotted the same, or different, levels of access privilege. The files may be stored in a particular system, also known as the server, and can be accessed by more than one user, depending on the levels of access privilege.

The user must keep the following points in mind while sharing a folder:

- Folders can only be shared, not files.
- Shared folders are only related to users who access the folder over a network, not users who locally log on to a computer.
- When a copy of a shared folder is taken, only the original folder is shared, not the copied one.
- When a shared folder is moved from its original position, the folder will lose its sharing attribute.

Types of File Sharing

A *default share* is a type of folder sharing that requires no configuration apart from the share designation. These types of shares can be created locally, or on a network. All users of the local machine can have access to the shared folder if the user sets a default local share. When the user sets a default network share in a workgroup setting, all users in the workgroup can access the files.

A *restricted share* is a type of folder sharing that contains more restrictions than a default share. This type of share can be created locally, or on a network. The user can restrict the number of users who can access the share at a particular given time. The user is also allowed to designate specific users who can access the share, and allot permissions to control user activity on the share.

How to Share a Folder

Follow these steps to share a folder:

1. Right-click the folder to be shared, and click **Properties**.
2. Click the **Sharing** tab in the folder properties dialog box.
3. Click **Share this folder**, and then in **Share name**, type the name of the folder to be shared.
4. If the user types the folder name with the $ symbol, the folder is shared, but does not appear when users browse for it across a network.
5. In **Comment**, type a description for the shared folder. This description is visible to users who browse across a network.
6. In **User limit**, the user can make any changes required.
7. The default setting is **Maximum allowed**, which corresponds to the number of client access licenses you have purchased.
8. The user can also designate a user limit by clicking **Allow**, typing the number of users next to **Users**, and then clicking **OK**.

The shared folder permissions are set to Everyone group with Full Control permission. The user can also share a folder from the command prompt by using the **Net share** command.

Configuring Shared Folder Permissions

Follow these steps to set, view, change, or remove file and folder permissions:

1. Right-click the folder and click **Properties**.
2. In the folder properties dialog box, click the **Sharing** tab, and then click **Permissions**.
3. In the **Permissions for** dialog box, click **Add**.
4. In the **Select Users, Computers, or Groups** dialog box, click **Object Types**, click the **Users** check box, and then click **OK**.
5. Under **Enter the object names to select**, type the name of the group or user for which permissions need to be configured, and then click **OK**.
6. In the **Permissions for** dialog box, in the **Group or user names** box, click the group or user.
7. In the **Permissions for** dialog box, allow or deny permissions, and then click **OK**.

Chapter Summary

- Hardware requirements, such as network cards, cable, and signal distributors (hub or switch) must be determined before installing a network.
- Hubs forward data to all computers in a network; switches determine the MAC address of the recipient, and send data to the designated computer on a network.
- Computers and devices connected on a TCP/IP network are identified by a special 32-bit address called an IP address.

- Before assigning IP addresses in a network, it is necessary to verify the network connection.
- A workgroup allows easy sharing of network resources.
- The three most common network services are DHCP, WINS, and DNS.
- Network architecture, or topology, refers to the configuration of cables, computers, and other peripherals in a network.
- ISPs offer Internet connection by using specific data transmission technology appropriate for different Internet protocols.
- Sharing of data over a network is called file sharing.
- Types of folder sharing include a default share and a restricted share.

Review Questions

1. What are the hardware requirements that need to be determined before setting up a network?

2. What are the differences between a hub and a switch?

3. How are IP addresses categorized? Why?

4. What does a workgroup allow users in a small network to do?

5. Define the three network services discussed in this chapter.

6. What are the issues to be considered when deciding on a network architecture, or topology?

7. What are the different Internet access technologies offered by ISPs discussed in this chapter? What are the advantages of each?

8. What is file sharing?

9. How can shared file access be limited to users on a network?

10. Define the types of file sharing.

Hands-On Projects

1. Find the PCI slot in your computer.
2. Determine the IP address of your computer.
3. Enable folder sharing on your computer.
4. Configure shared folder permission on your computer.
5. Try to make a dial-up connection on your computer.

Chapter 6

Wireless Networking

Objectives

After completing this chapter, you should be able to:

- Understand the basics of wireless networks
- Understand the types of wireless networks
- Recognize the requirements of a wireless network
- Know how to set up a wireless network
- Know how to access a WLAN
- Understand the advantages and disadvantages of wireless networks

Key Terms

Access point   a piece of wireless communications hardware that creates a central point of wireless connectivity

Bluetooth   a standard devised for providing specification for low-power, short-range connectivity between mobile devices and the Internet

Directional antennas   radiate radio waves in a more constrained area than an omnidirectional antenna

IEEE 802.11   standard that specifies the technologies for wireless LANs

Infrared light   used to connect devices at a very close range, less than or equal to one meter

Omnidirectional antennas   radiate electromagnetic energy regularly in all directions

SSID   a unique identifier that is used to establish and maintain wireless connectivity

Temporal Key Integrity Protocol (TKIP)   an improvement to WEP contained in the current draft of IEEE 802.11

Wired Equivalent Privacy (WEP)   the original version of 802.11 incorporated a MAC-level privacy mechanism

Wired Equivalent Privacy algorithm   encryption method included in IEEE 802.11 standard

Wireless Application Protocol (WAP)   responsible for the delivery and presentation of Web content to handheld devices, such as mobile phones

Wireless local area network (WLAN)   WLAN technologies connect users within a local area. The area can be a corporate or campus building, or a public space, such as an airport

Wireless metropolitan area network (WMAN)   allow users to communicate wirelessly between different locations within a metropolitan area; the area can encompass a university campus or multiple offices in a city

Wireless personal area network (WPAN)   a short-range, ad hoc network, providing instantaneous connectivity to the user; generally known as Bluetooth

Wireless wide area network (WWAN)   connects notebooks and handheld computers to the Internet using digital cellular networks across far-reaching geographic areas

Case Study

John runs his family's business. He is always on the move. Meeting overseas clients, conducting road shows, and keeping track of daily sales are all daily routines for him. Recognizing his needs, John bought a laptop, which could help him stay in contact with his clients and workforce while traveling.

John had a problem, though. He had limited knowledge of wireless networks. He called his friend Richard, a network engineer, to meet over lunch. John carried his laptop to the restaurant. Richard was waiting for him in the lounge.

John explained his limited knowledge of wireless networks, listened carefully, and saw Richard in action. Using Network Wizard in Windows XP, Richard set up the wireless connection in John's laptop.

Introduction to Wireless Networking

This chapter gives an overview of wireless networking and different types of wireless networks. The hardware requirements of a wireless environment are explored, setting up and connecting to a wireless network is explained, and the advantages and disadvantages of wireless networking are discussed.

Wireless Networks

Wireless local area networks, or WLAN technologies, connect users within a local area. The area can be a corporate or campus building, or a public space, such as an airport. A mobile user can connect to a LAN through a wireless (radio) connection. A standard, *IEEE 802.11*, specifies the technologies for wireless LANs. The standard includes an encryption method, the *Wired Equivalent Privacy algorithm*.

A wireless LAN offers a feasible way to provide data connectivity to an existing building where wiring may not be practical due to construction design, location, or expense involved. Apart from offering mobility and freedom from location restraints, WLANs are gaining popularity due to their ease of use.

Typical problems associated with the physical aspects of wired LAN connections do not arise as frequently with a wireless network. However, WLANs do raise the issue of security due to certain inherent features, such as radio waves being easier to intercept than transmissions sent using physical wires.

The user authentication and data encryption system known as *Wired Equivalent Privacy, or WEP*, incorporates a MAC-level privacy mechanism, and is being used to address these issues, but falls short of providing adequate security. Another point to bear in mind is that each *access point* (a piece of wireless communications hardware that creates a central point of wireless connectivity in a Wi-Fi network) shares a fixed amount of bandwidth among all users on a first-come, first-serve basis.

Because one of the major benefits of wireless networking is user mobility, an important issue to consider is whether users can move seamlessly between access points without having to log in again and restart their applications. Seamless roaming is only possible if the access points have a way of exchanging information as a user connection is handed off from one to another.

Expanding the IEEE Standard

Starting as an extension technology for conventional, or wired, LANs, IEEE Standard 802.11 has grown into something much more capable, complex, and confusing. When it first came out in 1997, the WLAN standard specified operation at 1 and 2 Mb/s in the infrared, as well as in the license-exempt 2.4-GHz Industrial, Scientific, and Medical (ISM) frequency band. An 802.11 network in the early days used to have a few PCs with wireless capability connected to an Ethernet (IEEE 802.3) LAN through a single network access point. IEEE Standard 802.11 operates at higher speeds and in additional bands. With its growth, new issues have arisen for 802.11, such as security, roaming among multiple access points, and even quality of service. These issues are dealt with by extensions to the standard, identified by letters of the alphabet, and derived from the 802.11 task groups that created them.

802.11a

The 802.11a extension defines requirements for a physical layer (which determines the frequency of the signal and the modulation scheme to be used) operating in the Unlicensed National Information Infrastructure (UNII) band at 5 GHz, with data rates ranging from 6 Mb/s to 54 Mb/s. The layer uses a scheme called orthogonal frequency-division modulation (OFDM), which transmits data on multiple subcarriers within the communications channel. In many ways, it is similar to the physical-layer specification for HiperLAN II, the European wireless standard promulgated by the European Telecommunications Standards Institute.

802.11b

Commercially trademarked in 1999 by the Wireless Ethernet Compatibility Alliance (WECA) as Wi-Fi, this extension made 802.11b a household word. It defines operation in the ISM band at 5.5 Mb/s and 11 Mb/s (as well as the fallback rates of 1 Mb/s and 2 Mb/s). This physical layer uses the modulation schemes complementary code keying (CCK) and packet binary convolutional coding (PBCC). WECA is an industry organization created to certify interoperability among 802.11b products from diverse manufacturers.

802.11c

This task group's work on wireless LAN bridging has been folded into the 802.11 standard.

802.11d

This task group enhances the 802.11 specifications by spelling out its operation in new regulatory domains, such as countries in the developing world. In its initial form, the IEEE standard covered operation only in North America, Europe, and Japan.

802.11e

802.11 is used for real-time applications, like voice and video. To ensure that these time-sensitive applications have the network resources they need when required, this task group is working on adding mechanisms for ensuring quality of service to Layer 2 of the reference model, the media access control (MAC) layer. This layer controls which of several competing devices in a shared system gets to use the medium of communication at each instant of time. The current draft contains both statistical and deterministic mechanisms for differentiating traffic.

802.11f

802.11 implementations are evolving from small extensions of wired LANs into larger networks with multiple access points. These access points must communicate with one another to allow users to roam among them. This task group is working on extensions that enable communication between access points from different vendors.

802.11g

This task group is working on high-speed extensions to 802.11b. The current draft of 802.11g adopts OFDM from 802.11a, as well as two additional modulation schemes: PBCC and CCK-OFDM. The current draft of 802.11g enables data rates as high as in 802.11a (54 Mb/s). Development of this extension was marked by a great deal of contention in 2000 and 2001 over modulation schemes. A breakthrough occurred in November 2001, and the task group worked to finalize its draft during 2002.

802.11h

This task group is working on modifications to the 802.11a physical layer to ensure that 802.11a may be used in Europe. The task group is adding dynamic frequency selection and power control transmission, which are required to meet regulations in Europe.

802.11i

The original version of 802.11 incorporated a MAC-level privacy mechanism called Wired Equivalent Privacy (WEP), which has proven inadequate in many situations. This task group is busy with improved security mechanisms. The current draft contains an improvement to WEP called *Temporal Key Integrity Protocol (TKIP)* and a new mode that incorporates the advanced encryption standard (AES), which is widely used in the banking industry. 802.11a represents the third generation of wireless networking standards and technology. It was actually approved as a standard earlier than 802.11b, but it presented a greater engineering challenge and was delayed.

Types of Wireless Networks

Wireless networking permits users across long distances to establish communication using *infrared light*, which can be used to connect devices at a very close range (less than or equal to one meter), or radio signals as a medium. Devices preferable for a wireless network include laptops, desktop computers, PDAs, cellular phones, pagers, and pen-based computers. Wireless networks have given freedom to people who travel frequently, by connecting them to the Internet wherever they are.

Wireless networks follow the same hierarchy followed by wired networks. A wireless LAN refers to a small network comprised of three or more devices; the global wireless network is known as the wireless Internet.

Wireless networks can be divided into four categories:

1. *Wireless Local Area Network (WLAN)*: WLAN technologies connect users within a local area. The area can be a corporate or campus building, or a public space, such as an airport.
2. *Wireless Personal Area Network (WPAN)*: It is a short-range, ad hoc network providing instantaneous connectivity to the user.
3. *Wireless Metropolitan Area Network (WMAN)*: WMAN technologies allow users to communicate wirelessly between different locations within a metropolitan area. An area can encompass a university campus or multiple offices in a city.
4. *Wireless Wide Area Network (WWAN)*: It connects notebooks and handheld computers to the Internet using digital cellular networks across far-reaching geographic areas.

WLAN

WLANs are local-area networks that use high-frequency radio waves, rather than wires, to communicate between nodes. They utilize either infrared light (IR) or radio frequencies (RF) for data transfer. WLAN setups employ spread spectrum technology, where electromagnetic energy generated in a particular bandwidth is spread in the frequency domain, providing signals with wider bandwidth. 802.11b, the new governing standard developed by IEEE, allows data transfer at a maximum rate of 11 Mbps over a 2.4-gigahertz (GHz) frequency band. 802.11a, a new emerging standard, specifies data transfer at a maximum rate of 54 Mbps over a 5-GHz frequency band.

WLANs work in two different modes. Infrastructure WLANs are wireless stations with radio network cards or external modems connected to wireless access points. These access points function as a bridge between the wireless stations and the existing network structure. Peer-to-peer or ad hoc WLANs allow users within a confined area, such as a conference room, to develop a temporary network without using access points if the users are not accessing network resources.

An in-building WLAN requires a PC Card client adapter installation, which gives wireless freedom to the user. It enables the user to roam freely within the coverage area, maintaining connectivity. For building-to-building WLANs, wireless bridges connect users without any license, and irrespective of any obstacle.

WPAN

A wireless personal area network interconnects devices within an individual person's workspace. WPAN technologies facilitate users in setting up ad hoc, wireless communications for devices such as PDAs, cellular phones, or laptops that are used within a space surrounding a person, ranging up to 10 meters. *Plugging in* and the ability to lock devices to prevent unauthorized access are two prime advantages of a WPAN.

The concept behind *plugging in* is that when two WPAN-equipped devices come in close proximity, they can communicate as if they are connected by a wired network. Each device in a WPAN can plug into another device equipped with the same WPAN if they are in physical range of each other.

Two key WPAN technologies widely used include **Bluetooth**, a standard devised for providing specifications for low-power, short-range connectivity between mobile devices and the Internet, and infrared light. Bluetooth is a cable replacement technology which exploits radio waves for data transmission up to a distance of 30 feet. Data can be passed through walls, pockets, and briefcases. The Bluetooth Special Interest Group (SIG) has taken the initiative to develop this Bluetooth technology and published the Bluetooth version 1.0 specification in 1999. On the other hand, infrared light can be used to connect devices at a very close range, less than or equal to one meter.

WMAN

A metropolitan area network interconnects users with computer resources in a region larger than a local area network, but smaller than the area covered by a wide area network. A wireless metropolitan area network (WMAN) serves as backup for wired networks. An emerging technology known as broadband wireless access networks are in great demand, connecting users with high-speed Internet.

Multichannel multipoint distribution services (MMDS) and local multipoint distribution services (LMDS) are in use today with WMANs. The IEEE 802.16 group, working on broadband wireless access standards, is evolving the standard for the development of this technology.

WWAN

Wireless wide area network (WWAN) technologies help users set up wireless connections over remote public or private networks. A WWAN connects the user with work-related information, even when away from the office. These connections can be established over large geographical areas, such as cities or countries. The medium for these connections consist of multiple antenna sites or satellite systems sustained by wireless service providers.

A WWAN is operated by a public carrier and requires licensing for data transmission. It employs open standards such as AMPS, GSM, TDMA, and CDMA. Modern WWAN technologies are known as second-generation (2G) systems. Key 2G systems incorporate Global System for Mobile Communications (GSM), Cellular Digital Packet Data (CDPD), and Code Division Multiple Access (CDMA).

A WWAN requires wireless modem and wireless structure for connectivity. The modem directly communicates with radio towers, which transmit the signal to a mobile switching center. From there, the signal is carried to a suitable public or private network link, which can be a telephone, other high-speed line, or even the Internet. From this network link, the signal can be passed to an organization's accessible network.

A universal specification, known as *wireless application protocol (WAP)* exists, which is responsible for the delivery and presentation of Web content to handheld devices, such as mobile phones. The request for Web content is made to a WAP gateway through the wireless network. A WAP gateway request is processed, and the required information is taken back and returned.

Wireless Network Requirements

Basically, four components make up a wireless network. They include Wi-Fi radio devices, access points, gateways, and a wireless network card. A wireless network card, which fulfills the Wi-Fi (IEEE 802.11b) standard for wireless networks, is required. It must operate in the 2.4-GHz spectrum, with a bandwidth of 11 Mbps (megabits per second).

The connections for a wireless network follow these steps.

First, the gateway is connected to the access point, the Internet, and a wired network, if the wired network is part of the network.

Next, Wi-Fi radio devices are connected to the gateway through the access points, where they can access the Internet. Wi-Fi equipped peripherals, including printers, scanners, cameras, video monitors, and set-top boxes, are emerging and will soon be commonplace.

Finally, an access point creates a central point of wireless connectivity and can be used to connect segments of a LAN using transmitting and receiving antennas, instead of ports, for access by multiple users of a wireless network. Similar to standard wired hubs, access points are shared bandwidth devices that can be connected to a wired network via a Network Access Medium (NAM), allowing wireless access.

Antennas

Antennas are very important for sending and receiving radio signals, converting electrical impulses into radio waves and vice versa. Directional and omnidirectional antennas are the two basic categories of antennas.

Omnidirectional antennas radiate electromagnetic energy regularly in all directions. They usually radiate strong waves uniformly in two dimensions, but not as strongly in the third dimension. These antennas are effective for irradiating areas where the location of other wireless stations will vary with time. A good example of an omnidirectional antenna is the one used by radio stations. These antennas are very effective for radio signal transmission because the receiver may not be stationary, but can get the signal regardless of direction.

Directional antennas radiate the radio waves in a more-constrained area. They are not as versatile as omnidirectional antennas, but are useful for fixed locations. These antennas are used when the distance between transmitter and receiver is no more than a few hundred meters. The amount of information that can be transferred is high; the wavelength used in these antennas is very small (10^{-12} to 10^{-14}).

Created mostly for personal use, can antennas are also well known in the wireless community. These antennas are made up of basic household items, such as PVC pipe, all-thread washers, cheap copper tubing, a can, and some scrap cardboard.

SSIDs

The *SSID* is a unique identifier that is used to establish and maintain wireless connectivity. SSIDs act as a single shared password between access points and clients. Security concerns arise when the default values are not changed, since these units can then be easily compromised. A nonsecure access mode allows clients to connect to the access point using the configured SSID, a blank SSID, or an SSID configured as "any". Access points and all devices attempting to connect to a specific WLAN must use the same SSID. A device will not be permitted to join the BSS (basic service set) unless it can provide the unique SSID. Because an SSID can be sniffed in plaintext from a packet, it does not supply any security to the network. SSIDs provide a means for multiple access points to serve multiple networks while discriminating between packets. The SSID can be up to 32 characters long. Even if the access points of these networks are very close, the packets of the two are not going to interfere. Some common SSIDs include comcomcom, default SSID, Intel, Linksys, and Wireless.

Access Point Positioning

An access point is a piece of wireless communications hardware, which creates a central point of wireless connectivity. Similar to a hub, the access point is a common connection point for devices in a wireless network. Wireless access points must be deployed and managed in common areas of a network and should be coordinated with the telecommunications and network managers.

The following points should be kept in mind while positioning the access points:

- Access points in a WLAN should not be placed where the signal leaks out.
- Choose a location for access points that maximizes the broadcast pattern of the antenna over areas located inside the area where users will be located and not outside, or in nonuser areas.
- In order to reduce the amount of signal lost due to the cable between the antenna and access point, situate the device as close to the antenna as possible.
- Most access points are not waterproof, and need to be kept indoors.

Ideally, if the antenna is roof mounted, try to position the access point in the top floor of the building.

WEP

Wired Equivalent Privacy (WEP) is a security protocol, specified in the IEEE Wi-Fi standard 802.11b, designed to provide a WLAN with a level of security and privacy comparable to what is usually expected of a wired LAN. Wired LANs typically employ physical controls to prevent unauthorized users from connecting to the network and viewing data. In a wireless LAN, the network can be accessed without physically connecting to the LAN. IEEE chose to employ encryption at the data-link layer to prevent unauthorized eavesdropping on a network. This is accomplished by encrypting data with the RC4 encryption algorithm.

Role of WEP in Wireless Communication

- WEP is protection for wireless communication against eavesdropping.
- WEP prevents unauthorized access to a wireless network.
- WEP relies on a secret key that is shared between a mobile station and an access point, which is used to encrypt packets before they are transmitted. An integrity check is used to ensure that packets are not modified in transit.
- 802.11 WEP encrypts data only between 802.11 stations.

Setting Up a Wireless Network

Before installing a wireless LAN, it is necessary to confront the limitations and abilities of the wireless network hardware. For the installation of a WLAN, the foremost concern is finding the best location for an access point. Radio waves are used for communication in a WLAN, so it is essential that the access point be free from obstructions. It is best to mount an access point (AP) at a high level from the ground. Once that is done, the next step is connecting the AP and the rest of the equipment. If a standalone AP is going to be added to an existing Ethernet LAN, it is necessary to run an Ethernet cable from the AP to the existing network switch. If a combination router/firewall/AP device is installed, which will connect to a cable or DSL modem, run an Ethernet cable from the modem to the router, or move the modem so that it is close to the router.

Connecting an Adapter

For a wireless LAN, each wireless computer must have an adapter. There are various types of adapters such as PCI, USB, and Card Bus. A PCI adapter is difficult to install, but USB, Card Bus, and PC Cards are easy to install.

Follow these steps to install USB, PC Card, and Card Bus adapters:

1. Read the instructions packed with the desired adapter and install.
2. For USB adapters, plug the adapter into an unused USB port on the computer or USB hub.
3. For PC Card and Card Bus adapters, plug the card into an unused card slot on the computer.

Installing a Driver

After connecting the adapter, the next step is to install the drivers. Drivers can be installed using the Hardware Wizard in Windows.

Follow these steps to install a driver using the Hardware Wizard:

1. Turn on the computer and connect the adapter.
2. Insert the installation CD.
3. Select Install the Software Automatically, and click **Next**.
4. Windows automatically locates the correct driver. If Windows finds more than one possible driver, a prompt is given to choose the proper driver.
5. Choose the appropriate driver from the list, and click **Next**.
6. Installation is complete.

Before configuring the AP, establish the connection between a Web browser and the AP interface. Usually, the AP has a specific set of IP addresses that come in the private address range.

Follow these steps for configuring the AP:

1. Enter the IP address in the address bar of the browser.
2. The browser interface has a button marked **Run Wizard** that starts the setup wizard.
3. Set the password for the AP that is a combination of alphanumeric characters.
4. Set the name (called an SSID) and a channel name for the AP.
5. Enable the AP's encryption security feature.

6. Accept the settings applied and apply them to the AP.
7. If SSID settings are changed, reconfiguration is required; otherwise, configuration is completed.

These steps will install and configure at least one wireless PC to operate within the wireless network. If more PCs need to be installed, it is better to install them at the same time in the same manner.

Accessing a WLAN

Follow these steps to access a wireless LAN:

1. The computer should be enabled with a wireless network interface card (NIC), a card that has the circuitry to help the station get connected to a network.
2. The NIC should be placed with care in the slot assigned to it.
3. After the wireless NIC is placed in the slot, install the NIC driver with the help of the CD/floppy disk that came with the card from the manufacturer. In most cases, the operating system automatically detects the driver.
4. Configure the NIC to automatically set up its IP address, gateway, and DNS servers.
5. Use the software that came with the NIC to automatically detect the WLAN, and go online.
6. One of the ways to check if the system is online is to run an intrusion detection system.
7. An IDS sends alerts when the device gets any kind of network traffic.
8. An easier way to check if the system is online is to find the AP by running software, such as Wi-Fi Finder or NetStumbler.

Advantages and Disadvantages of Wireless Networks

There are pros and cons to using a WLAN for the home or office. The advantages include mobility for users to access their networks and ease of connection. Furthermore, the initial cost to set up a WLAN is low while manually cabling an entire enterprise will be expensive. Finally, data can be transmitted in different ways, making data sharing easy between wireless devices in a WLAN.

Mobility can also be the biggest disadvantage in a wireless network, since there is no physical security. There is a high expense after implementation, and the risk of data sharing is high; the packets are sent through the air, allowing an attacker to easily sniff through data by using various wireless sniffing tools. The various methods of transmitting data wirelessly allow more ways to steal data. Also, most wireless networks use a broad spectrum; it is very easy to identify the signal, which makes it more vulnerable to hackers.

Chapter Summary

- The popularity gained by wireless technology is due to two primary factors—convenience and cost.
- WLANs use spread spectrum technology for communication in a coverage area.
- For a wireless network setup, Wi-Fi devices, gateways, an access point, and a wireless network card are prerequisites.
- The SSID is a unique identifier that is used to establish and maintain wireless connectivity.
- One of the ways to check if a system is online is to run an intrusion detection system.
- The initial cost to set up a WLAN is low; manually cabling an entire enterprise can be expensive.
- The risk of data sharing is high in WLANs; data packets are sent through air, and an attacker can easily sniff through the air using various wireless sniffing tools.
- Positioning the access point is a crucial factor in a wireless setup.

Review Questions

1. What is the IEEE standard that specifies the technologies for WLANs?

2. What is an access point (AP)?

3. What wireless issues are addressed in the extensions to the IEEE standard?

4. What four categories represent wireless networks?

5. What is spread spectrum technology?

6. What is Bluetooth technology?

7. What are the hardware components for a wireless network?

8. Describe the two basic categories of antennas.

9. What is an SSID, and what is its major weakness?

10. What is the role of WEP in wireless communication?

11. What are the advantages of a wireless network? What are the disadvantages?

Hands-On Projects

1. Find the access point for your classroom.
2. Try to set up a WLAN connection.
3. Compare the data transfer speed of a wireless network to a wired network.
4. Add a laptop to a WLAN.

Chapter 7

Networking Environment

Objective

After completing this chapter, you should be able to:
- Define an intranet
- Understand the difference between the Internet and an intranet
- Understand how an intranet operates
- Follow a checklist for building an intranet
- Know the difference between the Internet and an extranet
- Understand how an extranet operates

Key Terms

Distributor extranet   provides hierarchy of authorization to various individuals, based on the size of the dealings

Extranet   a network that connects different intranets together through the Internet; it enables the linking of intranets of business partners, suppliers and researchers, or different intranets belonging to a central management

Intranet   a private network used within an enterprise, it contains different interlinked local area networks and exploits leased lines for a wide area network

Peer extranet   encourages on-par competition between different companies in the business sector by connecting small and large companies to share product prices and specifications

Supplier extranet   maintains the requisite level of stocks in the inventory and facilitates the workflow by connecting the store branches to their central store

Case Study

Nora, a final-year science student, is curious to know the architecture of her university's intranet. She approaches the network administrator of her school, who explains the institution's configuration of intranet, extranet, and the Internet. Nora also realizes that the data transfer rate for the school's intranet is faster than the Internet. She is also shown the school's different intranet components.

Prior to her meeting with the network administrator, Nora is confused about the differences between an intranet Web server and a mail server.

Introduction to Networking Environment

This chapter presents an overview and compares different networking environments. Intranets and extranets, their differences to each other and the Internet, and how they operate, are discussed in detail. A checklist for building an intranet is also presented.

Introduction to Intranet

An *intranet* is a private network, which is utilized within an enterprise. It contains different interlinked local area networks and exploits leased lines for a wide area network. Companies utilize intranets to share information and computing resources between employees. Intranets also allow working in groups and teleconferencing.

An intranet is similar to a private version of the Internet. It utilizes TCP/IP, HTTP, and other protocols for data transfer. In an organization, users can access the public Internet through a firewall, which prevents the passage of a company's sensitive information and maintains security of an organization's data.

Managing an Intranet

If an organization is utilizing an intranet, it is necessary to manage it well. There are three ways of managing an intranet. The first option is to have a single, securely managed server, a program or computer that provides the resources or information to the other client terminals in a network. In this option, there is a single structured information architecture, in which only approved documents get posted, and a single designer controls the navigation. The second option is to have a mini Internet. Even with increased communication capacity, it falls short in coordinating information due to multiple online servers. The third option is to manage diversity. With this option, many servers are in use, but all Web pages follow a single set of templates and interface standards; this type of management enables a well-planned information infrastructure that facilitates navigation.

Internet and Intranet Differences

An intranet and the Internet are two different information environments, which follow their own user interface designs. There are different defining parameters, which help clarify the pros and cons of the Internet versus an intranet.

Intranet users are usually employees working in an organization who already possess much information about the organization. On the other hand, Internet users are usually the customers who surf the Web in the quest of information.

Employees perform routine tasks and complex applications that utilize the company's intranet. However, the company's Internet site is mainly used by the customer to find information.

The Internet has information on every topic that can be researched by the user. A company's intranet is usually limited to reports, human resource information, and other detailed data related to the organization.

There is a plethora of information available on the Internet, but an organization's intranet only contains related documents and resources.

A company's intranet is faster than most Internet Web browsers, allowing the user to access rich graphic, multimedia, and other advanced content. The Internet has low or medium bandwidth, which slows down information transmission.

Intranet Advantages

An intranet has an edge over other types of computer networks, because the technology is driven by the Internet's technologies and protocols, which are designed to be platform-independent. It enables the user to access information wherever needed, no matter what kind of computer is used (PC, Mac, etc.). The only prerequisite for the user's computer is Web browser software.

Intranets are gaining popularity because they are easy to set up and less expensive to maintain than traditional networks. Also, documents on an intranet are written in HTML, and can be saved as Web pages.

An intranet is faster than the Internet; this feature enables users to use graphics, sound, video, e-mail, and newsgroups with ease. It is not only perfectly suited for document sharing but provides a platform for data sharing (financial, resource planning, customer, etc.) across an organization. There are a variety of Web server technologies that enable Web pages to display and manipulate database content. This capability of an intranet can be utilized by employees to generate monthly sales reports, research potential customers, reserve a conference room, or review production schedules.

In addition to data sharing, collaborative computing is also feasible with the use of an intranet. A genre of Web-based technologies allows employees to teleconference, Web-conference, chat, and share project planning resources across an intranet. This use of an intranet can wipe out geographic boundaries, scheduling limitations, and reduce travel costs.

How an Intranet Operates

In addition to delivering Web pages, there are many other technologies that use the same group of protocols. These technologies that carry out different tasks on an intranet are generally referred to as Internet applications, or *Web services*.

An intranet can be configured to:

- Utilize PPP (point-to-point protocol) to enable users to dial in.
- Provide e-mail services.
- Allow file transfer with FTP.
- Execute newsgroup services.

The basic architecture of an intranet consists of three components: a TCP/IP-enabled network, Web servers, and Web clients or browsers. For communication, each computer on a network has its unique IP address. Similarly, computers on an intranet are assigned network identification names, which allow the transfer of data from one computer to another. When a Web server is installed on a computer linked to a TCP/IP network, other computers on the network are able to request Web pages from the server by entering the server computer's network identification name into their browser's address bars. For example, the server computer's name is snick01 and a file in the Web server's HTML directory is called HomePage.html. The users on the network will be able to access that page by typing http://snick01/HomePage.html into their browser's address bar. When a computer's name without a path and filename is entered into a Web browser's address bar, the queried computer typically responds by sending its default Web page. Most default pages recognize the genre of server on which they start. Most often, many Web servers are designed to send pages called index.htm or home.htm when a user requests just the host name. See Figure 7-1 for the typical components within an intranet.

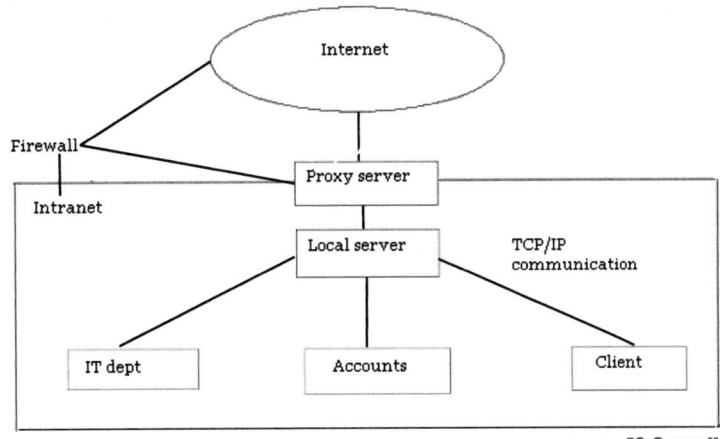

Figure 7-1 An example of the components found in a company intranet.

Inside an Intranet

Before installing an intranet, make a list of all components that are required. This list must include:

- *IP network*: The network comprising the network-layer protocol, which allows connectionless transmission of data packets; it is connected through devices such as routers and gateways.
- *HTTP server*: A server dedicated to retrieving Web documents.
- *SMTP/POP3/IMAP4 server*: A server using TCP/IP protocol for electronic mail services on the Internet.
- *LDAP Server*: A server that maintains LDAP (Lightweight Directory Access Protocol), an Internet protocol, utilized by e-mail programs to look up contact information from a server.
- *X509 Certificate Server*: An X509 certificate server, which authenticates the digital signatures.
- *Java ORB (Object Request Broker)*: Used for client-server applications on the Web.
- *Document server*: Used for dynamically generating documents in the required format, such as PDF.

Features of an intranet can include:

- A discussion board, which promotes the sharing of ideas in the absence of face-to-face discussions; it also encourages communication between departments and peer groups that might not normally share information.
- A Web mail application, to enable downloading of mail automatically and manually.
- Knowledge management, to facilitate knowledge synthesis, production, and exchange in order to achieve the strategic goals of the organization.
- Information mapping, which details the necessary information related to a company, such as policies, procedures, manuals, and marketing information.
- Document sharing, to enable data sharing of documents that are controlled by a rights management system to ensure check-in and check-out of documents to preserve sensitive information.
- Workflow management, to automate the business processes among different divisions, such as expenses approved by managers.
- Video/voice conferencing, to allow the user to maintain relations, not only in the organization, but also outside the corporate structure; business can be conducted without going anywhere.
- Knowledge preservation, to employ the processes to confine, archive, and protect explicit and implied knowledge, and maintain accessibility to it; employees can access this knowledge whenever they encounter any problem.

Checklist for Building an Intranet

Eight specific issues must be addressed before building an intranet.

1. *Decide on infrastructure requirements*: In general terms, the network infrastructure implies a TCP/IP protocol suite, managed on a local area network or used as a gateway to the Internet. The physical infrastructure requirement may be a combination of token-ring networks, 10 megabit-per-second (Mbps) Ethernet, 100-Mbps Ethernet, FDDI and ATM networks, associated hubs and routers, and T-1 and T-3 lines linked directly to the Internet, or to an ISP. Determining what type of infrastructure is required and whether it needs to be expanded or not are among the deciding factors.
2. *Determine the server required*: There are a variety of Web servers available. Choose a server based on the hardware and software platforms to be supported, as well as the kind of performance needed.
3. *Choose a browser*: A browser is required for each desktop. It is not necessary that every browser support all elements of the HTTP protocol and HTML, so find out how the different browsers implement graphics, support style sheets, and display content.
4. *Decide how the intranet will be used*: Common uses of corporate intranets include several human resource applications, such as policy and benefit manuals, documentation, staff directories, and online job postings. Usage of an intranet also comprises collaborative computing applications, multimedia, and applications linked to sales and marketing functions.
5. *Resolve the applications required*: After deciding on the Web server and browser, the next thing to be determined is the applications to run, and what type of Web interface tools are required.

6. *Determine the firewall required and how to build it*: Protection of an intranet from the outside world is achieved by a firewall. Firewall selection is the key element by which all users will obtain or be denied access to information on an intranet. In addition to its the primary purpose to block the public from accessing the intranet, the firewall may also be used as a one-way service for employees to go from the intranet directly to the Internet.

7. *Determining the roles of the Webmasters*: Lacking proper understanding of the roles of the Webmasters can make it difficult to know if the Webmasters are performing the appropriate duties required by the job. It is necessary to define the various roles to ensure that the data that needs to be made available to users is, in fact, being made available. In some organizations, the Webmasters are strictly technical; in other organizations, the Webmasters have content responsibility, in addition to keeping the servers up and running.

8. *Providing training to the users*: Basic training of users for the deployment of an intranet needs to be provided to allow users to perform their day-to-day activities easily, such as putting content on the server.

Introduction to Extranet

An *extranet* is a network that connects different intranets together through the Internet. It enables the linking of intranets of business partners, suppliers, and researchers, or different intranets belonging to a central management. Extranets allow users to share information and give authorization to access some files and services, while protecting the privacy of each intranet site. Extranets emerged as a response to the requirements of partnerships in the business sector. These kinds of relationships between business partners are called B2B (business to business). These business partners want a network that will make it possible for them to exchange sensitive information through setting levels of network accessibility.

There are three types of extranets:

1. *Supplier Extranet*: A **supplier extranet** maintains the requisite level of stocks in the inventory and facilitates the workflow by connecting the store branches to their central store. In addition to services related to inventory control, a supplier extranet diminishes the possibility of refusing orders due to shortage of stocks.

2. *Distributor Extranet*: A **distributor extranet** provides hierarchy of authorization to various individuals, based upon on the amount of business being conducted. It not only provides services such as electronic order and automated settlements, but also includes the addition of new products and specifications.

3. *Peer Extranet*: A **peer extranet** encourages on-par competition between different companies in the business sector by connecting small and large companies to share product prices and specifications. It lends a hand to improve the product and services of a company, and in restricting monopoly.

Internet and Extranet Differences

The Internet is popular because of the abundance of information that it contains. Using a Web browser, such as Netscape Navigator or Microsoft Internet Explorer, permits an individual to access any information placed on public Web servers. This information is available in a wide range, from official government documents, statistics, and transcripts, to newspaper articles, magazine articles, and real-time stock market quotes. The only differentiating factors of the Internet are the public accessibility that it provides and a lack of security in data transmission. See Figure 7-2 for an illustration of security hierarchy of intranets, extranets, and the Internet.

For example, an organization that wants to link specific targets of companies or customers and provide specific types of information builds an extranet. The idea of an extranet has evolved to present a secure environment that the Internet lacks. An extranet is able to provide a secure environment in which suppliers, distributors, resellers, and/or customers can communicate online, give orders, track sales and inventory, and exchange any other sensitive information, which would otherwise not be feasible. An extranet can be protected by using the latest technology employed for authentication and security software, including firewalls.

Extranet Advantages

Extranets have played a vital role in the business-to-business area and provide tremendous benefits. The biggest advantage offered by extranets is their ability to secure the relationship between a business and all of its supply chain partners.

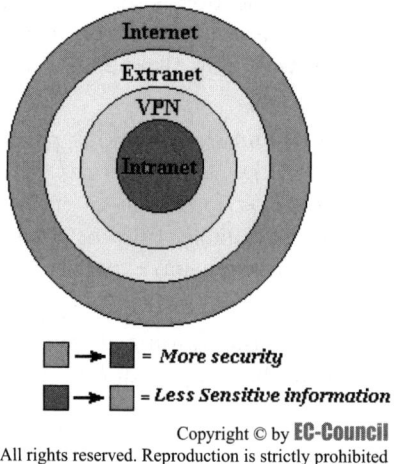

Figure 7-2 Different levels of security are offered for intranets, extranets, and the Internet.

The advantages of extranets include:

- *Decreasing the cost of goods*: Extranets enable online communication, eliminating many manual processes, paper, and faxes, which reduces costs at all levels of the supply chain. Ordering, handling paper, faxing, and tracking shipments represent a major portion of total operating expenditures.
- *Enhancing demand forecasting*: Extranets provide updated information to business partners, enabling sharing of up-to-the-minute demand forecasts and information related to production. This ability keeps business partners along the supply chain informed with the latest information.
- *Platform independence*: An extranet is driven by Internet technology, making it independent of any type of specific or administered platform. In generic terms, it eliminates compatibility barriers in connecting with others.
- *Quicker time to market*: An extranet allows companies to launch new products to markets at a much faster rate than ever before. It also facilitates a company's edge over others to match competitors' offerings more quickly. An extranet can prevent stockouts as well, which helps in increasing customer satisfaction.
- *Better knowledge of customers*: In a supply chain, consumer demands can rise so fast that the customer gets lost in the process, with manufacturers slow to respond. However, the emergence of extranets changes this scenario. By allowing a manufacturer to link directly into a distributor's order management system to get a better understanding of customer demand, they can help that distributor meet those demands in a more timely fashion. Extranets make it easier for manufacturers to produce the right products, at the right time, and at the right price, improving customer satisfaction.

How an Extranet Operates

In an extranet, as shown in Figure 7-3, an organization's intranet is connected to the Internet through a firewall. The purpose behind firewall installation is to provide protection against unauthorized access. Because the Internet provides public accessibility, data transmission is not secure. That is why, to confront this problem, many organizations use *tunneling* technology to create a secure pathway for their data. Tunneling ensures protection of data from decoding by hackers. This protection is very important from a business and private data transmissions point of view.

Another extranet architecture can be one in which organizational intranets are linked through a *direct leased line*. This method is now favored over other methods for providing enhanced security and reliability to the

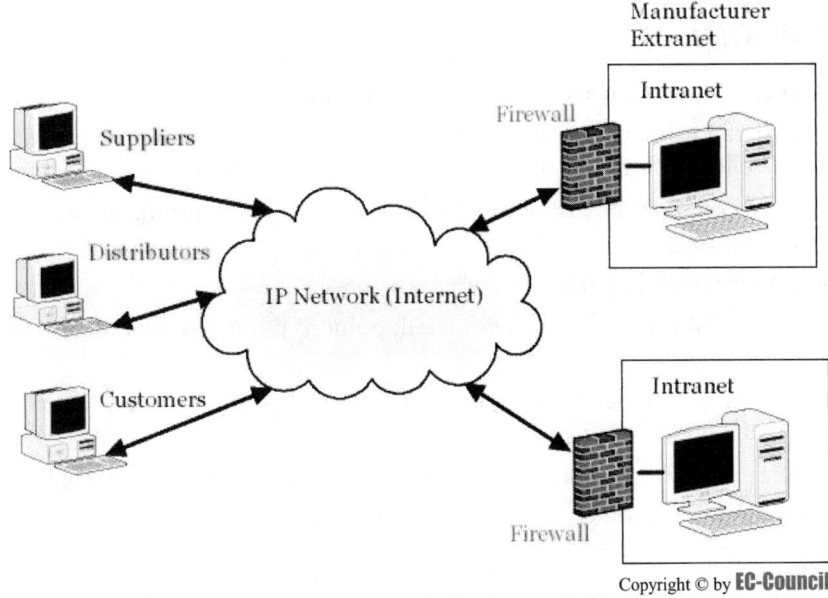

Figure 7-3 Firewalls provide protection against unauthorized access between intranets and the Internet in an extranet environment.

Intranet	Extranet
It is a private network used for sharing information in organizations.	It permits individuals from distinct organizations to access resources available on an intranet.
It increases the efficiency and communication in the various areas of an organization such as sales, finance, and human resources.	It is a business-to-business tool allowing communication between clients, partners, and distributors.
It provides secure, customized access to relevant information.	It not only provides data but also conducts electronic commerce.
It is restricted to internal data sharing.	It facilitates internal, as well as external, data sharing.

Table 7-1 Extranets allow a controlled expansion of separate business intranets to permit internal and external data **sharing**

connection. Using direct leased lines provides protection for a group's extranet, utilizing a controlled network to secure the connection. Security must be a priority because direct leased lines are expensive.

Another potential method of establishing an extranet architecture makes intranet content freely available on the Internet. It is similar to working with mirrored sites, in which a Web server, connected to the Internet, mirrors the content of an internal intranet Web server. This type of extranet is suitable for a network that does not need to carry sensitive business and private data transmissions. The URL of this extranet site would be provided only to employees and approved partners.

Intranet and Extranet Differences

See Table 7-1 for a contrast of the differences between an intranet and an extranet.

Chapter Summary

- An intranet is a private network used within an enterprise.
- An intranet can be managed three ways; a single server, a mini Internet, and multiple servers with Web pages that follow a single set of templates and interface standards.
- Intranets and the Internet are two different information environments, which follow their own user interface designs.
- An intranet is faster than most Internet browsers.
- Intranets offer Web services, such as e-mail, point to point protocol to allow users to dial in, file transfer with FTP, and newsgroup services.
- Computers on an intranet are assigned network identification names, which allow the transfer of data from one computer to another.
- An extranet is a network that connects different intranets together through the Internet.
- There are three types of extranets: supplier, distributor, and peer.

Review Questions

1. Why do companies use intranets?

2. What are some differences between the Internet and intranets?

3. Why do intranets have an edge over other types of computer networks?

4. What collaborative computing technologies are possible with an intranet?

5. What three components make up the basic architecture of an intranet?

6. List several features available on intranets.

7. What is an extranet?

8. Define the three types of extranets.

9. What makes the Internet different from an extranet?

10. What do firewalls provide in an extranet environment?

11. What are the differences between an intranet and an extranet?

Hands-On Projects

1. Determine if you are connected to your school's intranet. Justify your answer.
2. Identify the components in your school's intranet.
3. Identify the most commonly used features on your school's intranet.
4. Is your school's intranet connected to an extranet?

Chapter 8

Troubleshooting

Objectives

After completing this chapter, you should be able to:

- Recognize hardware errors and their codes
- Follow troubleshooting guidelines
- Understand how to test network connectivity
- Check for other common problems

Introduction to Troubleshooting

This chapter defines a set of strategies that can be used to define and resolve problems encountered while using information technology. General troubleshooting guidelines are discussed, as well as more specific issues, such as network connectivity and file/printer sharing. Failures of motherboards, CPUs, power supplies, video/displays, memory chips, and CD-ROMs are also presented, along with specific strategies for resolution.

Hardware Errors and Their Codes

Issues will arise when computer hardware and devices have communication problems. Error codes will signal which device is causing the problem; understanding these messages is vital to some resolution of an often complex process. Table 8-1 contains some of the most common error codes and their related messages.

Error code	Error Message
1	This device is not configured correctly.
18	Reinstall the drivers for this device.
19	Your registry might be corrupted.
31	This device is not working properly because Windows cannot load the drivers required for this device.
37	Windows cannot initialize the device driver for this hardware.
44	An application or service has shut down this hardware device.

Table 8-1 Common Error Codes and their Related Messages

Troubleshooting Guidelines

Troubleshooting can be defined as a set of strategies used to describe and resolve problems encountered while using information technology tools.

The following points should be kept in mind while troubleshooting:

1. It is hard to solve a problem if it cannot be defined. Define a problem by asking questions. Some examples of these questions follow:

   a. How often does this problem occur?

   b. Has any new hardware been installed recently?

   c. Have any modifications been made to the computer recently?

2. Look for common faults first, rather than complicated issues.

3. Always check for any error code on the screen.

4. Restart the computer to refresh system resources; the issue is sometimes resolved.

5. Confirm whether the problem is caused by hardware or software, and follow the necessary steps.

6. Read the service manual for the hardware/ software to troubleshoot the problem.

7. Finally, call technical support if all the previous steps fail.

Network Connectivity Issues

Network connectivity problems are common these days. Common reasons behind these problems include faulty network adapters, faulty switch settings, and issues related to hardware and drivers.

The first step is to check connectivity through the LAN cable; confirming proper connectivity often solves the issue. If the LAN cable seems to be unplugged, the user must replace the cable and recheck for connectivity.

Next, check whether TCP/IP is installed. In the absence of TCP/IP, the user will have to install TCP/IP.

Connectivity can also be checked by replacing a possible faulty network adapter with a tested one. To start, uninstall the network adapter diagnostics program and the existing card, found in network properties. Then, install the new network adapter.

Testing Network Connectivity

Network connectivity can be tested with the use of the Ping command in command prompt. The Ping command verifies connections to a remote computer or computers. This command is available only if the TCP/IP protocol has been installed.

To ping a network, the user must follow these steps:

1. Click **Start** → Click **Run** → type **cmd** → Click **OK**.

2. Type **Ping <IP address>**.

There are three possible responses to a Ping command. A reply message indicates connectivity. A request timeout message indicates that there is problem in connectivity. A destination host unreachable message indicates that the LAN cable is unplugged.

File and Printer Connectivity

These days, there may be multiple computers on a home network that need to be able to share files and printers. Follow these steps to verify computers for file and printer sharing.

1. Go to **Start** → **Settings** → **Control panel.**
2. Double-click **Network.**
3. Verify the listing of installed components for file and printer sharing.
4. Install by clicking **File and printer sharing.**
5. Grant access of your files to others.
6. Restart the computer.

Verify that file sharing is configured in the computer by checking the folder sharing setting.

1. Go to **Start** → **Run** → type **sysdm.cpl** → Click **OK.**
2. Check the computer name in the computer name tab.
3. Go to **Start** → **Run** → type **fsmgmt.msc** → Click **OK.**
4. Click **Share** to list the shared files and folders.

Check the log:

1. Go to **Start** → **Run** → type **%systemroot%\nsw.log** and press Enter.

File and printer sharing can also be configured by using Network Setup Wizard.

Motherboard Failure

Symptoms may appear on your computer that can indicate a motherboard failure. The computer may restart itself often or go dead in the middle of a Windows session. Windows may become unstable, with no specific or clear reason.

Windows may begin to report new error messages or fail to load at all, even when using Safe Mode; these problems may begin slowly and then increase. New devices may appear and disappear from BIOS or Device Manager.

Motherboard failures can be caused by physical damages due to mishandling during installations. Moving the PC case without protection from being hit or pushed, and bending the motherboard too severely during a difficult installation can cause physical damage.

Other reasons for failure can include a lightning strike or power surge while the computer is operating unprotected, extreme temperature or humidity, and a lack of servicing for long periods of time.

Response

The motherboard must be replaced if conditions such as burnt areas, melted wires, fractures, and warping are observed. Also, flickering or smoke coming from the motherboard can indicate a necessary replacement; a smoking power supply or component may not affect the motherboard unless you continue to run the PC with this problem.

There are a few motherboard handling tips that can promote safety and provide optimal operation. Position the motherboard so that the board does not touch the metal standoffs in the case, check for foreign substances or a large deposit of dust particles, and make sure that two pieces of metal are not touching each other. Also, wear an antistatic wrist strap while handling the motherboard. This safety measure helps in avoiding short circuits.

Central Processor Unit Failure

The only solution for a damaged central processor unit, or CPU, is to replace the CPU. If you get an error message relating to the CPU, follow these steps to check the status.

1. Turn off the PC, disconnect the power, and remove the cabinet cover.
2. Wear an antistatic wrist strap to protect you and your motherboard from short circuits.

3. Locate the CPU and check its seating. For a PGA-style CPU, make sure that the CPU is inserted properly into its socket. For an SECC-style CPU, ensure that the CPU is completely inserted into its slot.
4. Reconnect the power and try booting the CPU again.
5. Check the same for the CPU fan.

Checking the CPU Fan

The CPU fan is an important component of a computer; a faulty or nonoperational CPU fan can cause damage or even destroy a CPU. The CPU fan removes the heated air around the processor. This is crucial since heat can shut down a computer. Most of the motherboards available today include a thermal sensor feature that automatically shuts down a system when there is an increase in the interior temperature.

Power Supply Failure

The PC power supply is probably the most failure-prone part of a computer. Some symptoms of a power supply failure include a stalled cooling fan that can overheat components and a burning smell when the computer shuts down. Random rebooting or failure in Windows without a specific reason can also be a symptom of power supply failure.

Usually, a power supply either dies slowly, or immediately and forever. It can even fail in the middle of a session. In most cases, your computer would switch off and not restart, even if you try to turn it on again. If it does start, you might smell smoke or overheated parts.

If a fan gets stuck, turn the computer off and disconnect the power. Use a can of compressed air to clear debris and dust from the fan. Apply grease frequently to the fan's blades to enable smooth operation. The fan should not be reinstalled until it is fully cleaned and dry; use extreme care when reattaching the fan into the power supply and all the connectors from the power supply to the other parts of your system.

Video/Display Failure

Some people assume that when they switch on their computer power supply and fail to see a display, then there is something wrong with the video itself. However, this can be a symptom of any kind of failure. But, there are some common reasons for a video/display failure.

The monitor may not be plugged in to a proper power source. There may be loose or disconnected cables between the monitor and video adapter.

Less common failures can include a problem with the display driver, a video card not properly installed or configured, or a defective monitor. Also, the pins present in the cable that connects the monitor to the video adapter may be bent.

Finally, a damaged motherboard can also be a reason for video/display failure, especially if the video chip is integrated into the motherboard, rather than located on a separate add-in expansion board.

Memory Chip Failure

The symptoms for memory chip failure can include continuous beeps and the system failing to boot. An increase in the number of fatal exception errors, especially after a clean format and install, is a clear prediction of memory chip failure.

Troubleshooting for memory chip failure can include checking the chip for displacement and placing it back properly in its slot. If the problem persists, the final solution is to replace the damaged memory chip with a good one.

CD-ROM Failure

The most common and prevalent symptom of CD-ROM failure is the CD drive letter completely disappearing from My Computer. Troubleshooting should include checking to see if the light present on the drive glows when the system reboots, and if any data cable is loose or disconnected. To cross-check the status of the CD-ROM, see if the drive is accessible from DOS. If the CD drive still does not work, then the user can try booting with a Windows rescue floppy to enable the CD drive.

Chapter Summary

- Troubleshooting can be defined as a set of strategies used to describe and resolve problems encountered while using information technology tools.
- Confirm whether the problem is caused by hardware or software, and follow the necessary steps.
- Check network connectivity by replacing a faulty network adapter with a tested one.
- The Ping command verifies connections to a remote computer or computers.
- A symptom of motherboard failure is when Windows begins to report new error messages or fails to load at all when using Safe Mode; these problems may begin slowly and then increase.
- The only solution for a damaged CPU is to replace the CPU.
- Power supplies usually either die slowly, or immediately and forever, and can fail even in the middle of a session.
- A damaged motherboard can be a reason for video display failure, especially if the video chip is integrated into the motherboard, rather than located on a separate add-in expansion board.
- Troubleshooting for memory chip failure can include checking the chip for displacement and placing it back in its slot properly.
- The most common and prevalent symptom of CD-ROM failure is the CD drive letter completely disappearing from My Computer.

Review Questions

1. What does error code 1 mean?

2. List six guidelines to follow when troubleshooting.

3. What are the most common network connectivity problems?

4. How do you test network connectivity?

5. What symptoms may appear on your computer that would indicate a motherboard failure?

6. When should a motherboard be replaced?

7. Why do you need to wear an antistatic wrist strap when handling a motherboard?

8. How do you check the status of a CPU?

9. Why is the CPU fan so important to optimal functioning of a system?

10. What is the most failure-prone part of a computer?

11. What would indicate a power supply failure?

12. What are some common reasons for a video/display failure?

13. How would you troubleshoot a memory chip failure?

14. What is the most common symptom of CD-ROM failure?

15. What are the troubleshooting steps for CD-ROM failure?

Index

A

Access points, 6-2
Advanced technology attachment, 4-5
Arithmetic and logic unit (ALU), 4-2
Attachment unit interface (AUI), 3-4
ATX, 4-3

B

Baseband, 3-3
Baseband Ethernet, 3-4–3-5
Basic hardware components
   CPU installation, 4-3
   explained, 4-3
   floppy and CD/DVD drives installation, 4-5
   hard drive installation, 4-4–4-5
   hardware device detection, 4-10–4-11
   introduction to installation of, 4-2
   legacy devices, 4-5–4-9
   motherboard installation, 4-3–4-4
   power supply installation, 4-4
   understanding ports, 4-9–4-10
BIOS (basic input/output system), 4-2, 4-8–4-9
Bluetooth, 6-5
Bridges, 2-3
Broadband, 3-3
Broadband cable, 5-9
Broadband Ethernet, 3-5
Brouters, 2-5

C

Carrier Sense Multiple Access/Collision Detection (CSMA/CD), 3-3
CATV (Community Antenna Television), 3-6
CD drives, 4-3, 4-5
CD-ROM, failure, 8-4
Central processing unit (CPU)
   defined, 4-2
   failure, 8-3–8-4
   installing, 4-3
Client, 1-3
Client-server model, 1-4

CMOS (complementary metal oxide semiconductor), 4-4, 4-9
Coaxial cable, 2-5, 3-6
Connectors, 4-10
Control unit, 4-2

D

Data cables, 4-9
Default share, 5-9–5-10
Device Manager, 4-6
Dial-up connection, 5-9
Directional antennas, 6-6
Direct memory access (DMA), 4-6–4-7
Distributor extranet, 7-5
Domain Name Service (DNS), 5-6
DVD drives, installing, 4-5
Dynamic Host Configuration Protocol (DHCP), 5-5–5-6

E

Ethernet
   baseband, 3-4–3-5
   broadband, 3-5
   cable types, 3-5–3-7
   categories in, 3-3
   characteristics of, 3-2–3-3
   defined, 3-2
   LANs, 3-7
   physical characteristics, 3-3
Extranet
   difference between Internet and, 7-5–7-6
   difference between Intranet and, 7-7
   introduction, 7-5
   operation of, 7-6–7-7

F

Fast Ethernet, 3-7
Fiber-optic cable, 2-5, 3-6–3-7
File sharing, 5-9–5-10
Floppy drives, 4-3, 4-5

G

Gateways, 2-5, 6-5
Gigabit Ethernet, 3-7

H

Hard drive
   defined, 4-3
   installing, 4-4–4-5
Hardware devices, detecting, 4-10–4-11
Hardware errors, 8-1, 8-2
Hubs, 2-2

I

IDE/ATA devices, 4-7–4-8
IEEE 1394, 2-6, 2-7
IEEE 802.11, 6-2, 6-3–6-4
Infrared light, 6-4
Input/output (I/O) addresses, 4-6, 4-7
Integrated drive electronics (IDE), 4-5
Internet
   difference between Extranet and, 7-5–7-6
   difference between Intranet and, 7-2–7-3
Internet access technology, 5-7–5-9
Interrupt request lines (IRQs), 4-6
Intranet
   difference between Extranet and, 7-7
   difference between Internet and, 7-2–7-3
   introduction, 7-2
   operation of, 7-3–7-5
IP address, 5-3–5-4, 5-5, 5-6, 5-7

J

Jumpers, 4-3

L

LAN technologies
   baseband Ethernet, 3-4–3-5
   broadband Ethernet, 3-5
   connecting to VPN using Windows 2000, 3-8
   Ethernet and, 3-2–3-3
   Ethernet cable types, 3-5–3-7, 3-7
   Ethernet categories, 3-3
   introduction, 3-2
   physical characteristics, 3-3
   virtual private network (VPN), 3-7, 3-8

Legacy devices, 4-5–4-9
Linear bus topology, 1-7
Local area network (LAN), 1-4–1-5

M

Mainframe, 1-4
Media connectors, 2-6
Memory chip, failure, 8-4
Mesh topology, 1-6–1-7
Metropolitan area networks (MANs), 1-6
Motherboard
    defined, 4-2
    failure, 8-3
    installing, 4-3–4-4
Multimode fiber (MMF), 3-7

N

Network components, 2-1–2-5
Network connectivity, 8-2–8-3
    connecting computers, 5-2–5-3
    deciding on network architecture, 5-7
    file sharing, 5-9–5-10
    Internet access technology, 5-7–5-9
    IP addressing, 5-3–5-4, 5-5, 5-6, 5-7
    network services, 5-5–5-6
    setting up small network, 5-2
Network interface cards (NICs), 3-4, 6-8
Networks
    components of, 1-3
    defined, 1-2
    introduction to foundations of, 1-2
    models of, 1-3–1-4
    need for, 1-2–1-3
    topologies, 1-6–1-8
    types of, 1-4–1-6
    types of cables for, 2-5
Network topology, 1-6

O

Omnidirectional antennas, 6-6

P

PCI, 5-2
Peer extranet, 7-5
Peer-to-peer networks, 1-3–1-4

Ports, 4-9
Power supply
    defined, 4-2
    failure, 8-4
    installing, 4-4

R

RAM (random access memory), 4-3
Repeaters, 2-2
Restricted share, 5-10
Ring topology, 1-6, 1-7
RJ-11, 2-6
RJ-45, 2-6
Routers, 2-3, 2-4

S

SCSI, 4-8
Server, 1-3, 7-2
Shielded twisted-pair (STP), 2-5
Singlemode fiber (SMF), 3-7
SOHO (small office/home office), 5-2
SSIDs, 6-6
Star topology, 1-7, 1-8
Supplier extranet, 7-5
Switched Ethernet, 3-7
Switches, 2-4

T

Temporal Key Integrity Protocol (TKIP), 6-4
10Base2, 3-4
10Base5, 3-4
10BaseT, 3-4–3-5
10Broad36, 3-5
Thicknet, 3-4, 3-6
Thinnet, 3-4, 3-6
Transreceiver, 3-3
Tree bus topology, 1-7, 1-8
Troubleshooting
    CD-ROM failure, 8-4
    central processor unit failure, 8-3–8-4
    guidelines, 8-2
    hardware errors and their codes, 8-1, 8-2
    introduction, 8-1
    memory chip failure, 8-4

motherboard failure, 8-3
network connectivity issues, 8-2–8-3
power supply failure, 8-4
video/display failure, 8-4
Twinax, 3-6
Twisted-pair cable, 3-6

U

Unshielded twisted pair (UTP), 2-5
USB (Universal Serial Bus), 2-6, 2-7

V

Video/display, failure, 8-4
Virtual private networks (VPNs)
    connecting to, using Windows 2000, 3-8
    defined, 3-7

W

Wide area networks (WANs), 1-6
Windows Internet Name Service (WINS), 5-6
Wired Equivalent Privacy (WEP), 6-2, 6-6–6-7
Wired Equivalent Privacy algorithm, 6-2
Wireless application protocol (WAP), 6-5
Wireless Local Area Network (WLAN), 6-2, 6-4
Wireless Metropolitan Area Network (WMAN), 6-4, 6-5
Wireless networks
    advantages and disadvantages, 6-8
    explained, 6-2–6-4
    introduction, 6-2
    requirements, 6-5–6-7
    setting up, 6-7–6-8
    types of, 6-4–6-5
Wireless Personal Area Network (WPAN), 6-4–6-5
Wireless technology, 5-9
Wireless Wide Area Network (WWAN), 6-4, 6-5
Workstation, 1-3

X

xDSL, 5-8

Z

Zip drives, 4-3